From Failure to Financial FITNESS

C. Pete Benson & Dan Benson

DEDICATION

This book is ***dedicated*** to Pete's and Ginnie's parents, Jimmy and Frances Benson and Beverly and Belva Brown, for their incredible example, guidance, and Godly influence on our lives and the lives of their grandchildren and great grandchildren. Their love for God, family, and their integrity, hard work, and character will be felt and evidenced for many generations. It is because of them, this book could come to fruition and enjoyed by you and your loved ones.

C. Pete Benson and Dan Benson

CONTENTS

ACKNOWLEDGMENTS

Writing a book is not something you can do without many others helping you. Special thanks to the following individuals who assisted and invested in the completion of this book:

I (Pete) would like to thank my wife, Ginnie, for her patience, input, expertise, editing, and hours of listening and sacrifice she gave to this writing. Dan thanks his wife Mandy and children Kayleigh, Connor, and Imogen for time they had to spend alone while he was busy writing his sections of this book. Mandy especially had to endure Dan's many late nights and early mornings of thinking, typing, researching, and texting back and forth with co-author, Pete (Dad).

This truly has been a family project as Pete and Ginnie's daughters, (Dan's sisters) Ginger and Amanda, have also contributed greatly by reading, editing, and advising. A very special thanks additionally goes to Ginnie's sister, Pat Brown, as she invested many hours of editing for Pete and Dan's book.

Kristin Llamas deserves a huge amount of credit and applause for her expertise in book cover design, tweaking, publishing, and advising Pete and Dan on this project. She is so talented and a joy to work with.

It just wouldn't be right not to mention my business partner Jon Maxson. In ways he will never know or be given credit for, he adds value to my life, Dan's life, and our business and financial life. Many of the principles of this book have been learned and practiced together over the past 16 years as we have worked together.

PRAISE FOR THIS BOOK

"Pete Benson is a solid, informed, wise and proven voice of highly-valued counsel on personal financial matters. Having demonstrated the "failure to fitness" principles in his own life, he has earned a platform from which to share these principles with others. I am pleased to endorse and recommend this book to you. Read on!"

Dr. H.C. Wilson
General Superintendent Emeritus
The Wesleyan Church

"Compelling personal experiences both failure and success combined with sound advice make this brief book a "page-turner." This book spans all ages with specific actions and direction for each age group even well into retirement. Many fresh, new nuggets of truth not found in other books! A must for ALL!"

Dr. Jo Anne Lyon
Ambassador, General Superintendent Emerita
The Wesleyan Church

"Pete and Dan Benson have done us a great favor. They have provided advice that is practical, yet thorough, and anchored in biblical wisdom. No treatment of money would be complete without a chapter on giving and theirs is one of the best you'll find anywhere. What I appreciate most about this book is knowing that these men live what they 'preach.' Their advice is born from experience. No wonder it makes such good sense."

Dr. Steve Lennox,
President, Kingswood University

"Pete Benson's story inspires me. Now he shares the financial principles that have been foundational in that story. From a lifetime of study and personal experience, Pete shares timely information, biblical and inspirational that will motivate you to take your next step to financial freedom. Buy an extra copy for someone you care about because this book could be the key to changing their financial future. You'll enjoy it and they'll thank you!"

Dr. Mark Gorveatte
Author of *Lead Like Wesley*

"One of my favorite stories in the Bible is the Parable of the Five Talents in Matthew 25 which says we should make the most of what we are given. In their new book, Pete and Dan teach you how to maximize what you've been blessed with. I've known Pete for over 6 years, and he's what I call a Five Talent leader – he is a good and faithful servant – and in this book, you can learn the lessons that he teaches that lead to financial success. Read it, but more importantly, apply it!"

Cody Foster
CEO, owner, Advisors Excel

"Finally, a book has arrived, overflowing with practical financial counsel and biblical wisdom. The Bensons have captured, in this one resource, a way to have a relationship with money that brings freedom and hope like never before."

Dr. Todd Voss
President of Southern Wesleyan University

"My wife and I met Pete while we were financing an expensive international adoption on a very limited budget. Pete provided us with invaluable tools that not only helped us *expand* our family, but also *sustain* our family *and* prepare for the future. My family represents a *global community* that has been profoundly affected by Pete's wisdom, innovation, and generosity. I am forever indebted to him."

Dr. Mike Tapper
Division of Religion, Southern Wesleyan University

"Pete Benson is uniquely qualified to write this book. Not only is he an experienced and successful financial advisor but he has served in pastoral ministry and is a deeply committed Christian. This book is a clear, simple, and practical tool for moving from financial failure to experiencing the benefits of financial wisdom. This book is a quick read with results that will last a lifetime."

Russ Gunsalus
Executive Director of Education and Clergy Development
The Wesleyan Church

"Pete Benson combines his own compelling story with the necessary steps to create a financial future very different from a perilous past. Highly readable and thoroughly biblical, Pete takes us to the heart of the matter in a way that breathes hope into any situation."

Dr. Wayne Schmidt
General Superintendent, The Wesleyan Church

"An extraordinary work of Pete Benson CEO, author and consultant. In fact, it represents a lifelong collection of both personal study and practical experience with hundreds of individuals and organizations seeking financial health. This book can be the beginning of moving from financial failure to success within your life or organization. It is a valuable and easy read for all who seek to start this journey. "

Charles L. Joiner Ph.D
Consultant (Economics, Finance, Strategic Planning, Human Resource Management) Author, Higher Education Leadership

"From Failure to Financial Fitness, by my friend, C. Pete Benson, is an outstanding guide to financial freedom and prosperity. This book shares sage insights from a world class financial adviser and creates a pathway for making a meaningful and significant difference in the world!"

Mark O. Wilson,
Professor at Southern Wesleyan University, Pastor & Author

"Many of us feel like we have failed financially, or at least that we haven't done all we can to succeed with money. We can find the practical help we need in the straightforward wisdom of this book."

David Drury is the author of ten books, Chief of staff for the International headquarters of The Wesleyan Church.

"From Failure to Financial Fitness is exactly what you'd expect from Pete and Dan Benson – Truth spoken in love. If you are looking for practical advice to achieve financial peace-of-mind through a biblical lens, this is your book! Pete and Dan use this writing to reflect on the practical, biblical financial disciplines that have brought their family financial security and has made Beacon Capital Management one of the nation's top investment advisory firms."

D. Scott Rhyno
Chief Development Director – The Wesleyan Church, Indianapolis, Indiana

"When you meet a person who aligns personal passion with practical wisdom, great things happen! Pete is able to meet people where they are and lead them to freedom and possibility using scripture and experience. His ministry and writings are characterized with hope. I highly recommend anything associated with Pete Benson!"

Tom Harding
Sr. Pastor, Alive Wesleyan church, Central, SC

"Pete Benson is an exceptional communicator and if possible even more exceptional are his challenging, convicting and convincing insights regarding financial freedom. Everyone will be helped and desperately need these proven principles, especially those beginning a career."

Dr. Laurel D. Buckingham
CEO, Buckingham Leadership Institute

PREFACE

Entrepreneur, author, and motivational speaker Jim Rohn once said, "Formal education will make you a living, self-education can make you a fortune."[1] What makes no sense to me is how little practical financial education students receive in middle school, high school, or even in college. In both the United States and Canada there seems to be very little formal education on the subject of personal finances. And yet, it is something all of us need to know and implement for the rest of our lives. If we want to get the knowledge needed to make good sound financial choices for our lives, it seems to be all on our own shoulders. In other words, "self-education". It blows my mind that in high school, as a requirement to get credits for one course, I had to learn the rules of how to play badminton, and was even tested on it. And though that was 40 plus years ago, I've never played a game of badminton since I graduated high school. However, every single day, every week, every year of my adult life I have had to make impactful fiscal decisions and I don't remember any practical financial instruction given to me in high school or in my Bachelors' degree coursework. It wasn't until I took my Masters' degree that I had any formal teaching on personal finances.

Handling money is not a choice. You will handle it in your lifetime, either in a positive or a negative way. I love the Zig Ziglar quote, "money is not the most important thing in life, but it's reasonably close to oxygen on the 'gotta have it scale'"[2]

Have you ever been under water and the longer you stayed down there the more your lungs began to scream for oxygen? It can be a little scary and very uncomfortable for sure. In just a minute or two your lungs are desperate for air.

Have you ever been desperate for money? Likely the answer is yes. It is **yes** for me. You see, because of some selfish choices I made as a teenager, I ended up married and with a child before I finished grade 12. One minute I was a careless and carefree teenager and life was fun and games. I had no financial responsibility to speak of. The next thing I know, my young wife and I are 17-year-old "kids" with no education, no jobs, adult responsibility, a child to raise, and no idea where the money would come from to finance all this. We felt desperate. The best thing we did was turn our lives completely over to Jesus Christ. We had made a complete mess of everything, but perhaps He could make beauty out of ashes; (and a few loaves and fish would be awfully nice also). We did finish high school, thanks to our great family helping out in a big way. Then it was on to college; 18 years old and a child onboard. No money, no job, no tuition funds, no scholarships, but we had hope and a lot of prayer. It was at this point I realized I needed some education on personal finances, so I went to the local library and found some books to read to get practical instruction on what to do and how to do it. I needed all the help I could get! I read book after book on this subject and took useful notes. As well, I began to implement the ideas that made the most sense. In our first 10 years of marriage I read over 30 books on personal finance. I began to get a real passion for this and it really became a game. I quickly learned that it's not how much money comes in (income) as it is what you do with it and how you use it, spend it, and invest it (outgo). In other words, if you are doing dumb things with your money, having more isn't the answer. I like another of Jim Rohn's quotes, "If someone is going down the wrong road, he doesn't need motivation to speed him up. What he needs is education to turn him around."[3]

In addition to the 30 plus books I read, I also searched the Bible for instruction and inspiration. Guess what? I found a lot of very practical material on how to handle finances and possessions. In fact, I am told that there are 2350 verses in the Bible on the subject of money, possessions, and generosity. That would be more than prayer, faith, heaven, and hell combined. A large percentage of Jesus' teaching was on this subject. And let's not forget the book of Proverbs; there is so much practical financial instruction there!

Here's something else significant to keep in mind: being financially fit isn't just about information, it's about implementation. Many people know what to do, they just don't do it! It's not so much about **dollars** as it is about **discipline.**

This book is written as a practical handbook and overview on personal finances. We sure hope you enjoy it and more importantly we pray it changes your financial picture for the better, to the glory of God.

Mark Twain once said, "the secret to getting ahead is getting started",[4] so let's go!

I. PARTNER WITH GOD

"The earth is the Lord's and everything in it, the world, and all who live in it" **Psalms 24:1**... Now, re-read that verse out loud. Do you believe what it says? Do your actions with your finances reflect the fact that everything in this world is the Lord's? I have heard many people I have tons of respect for say this at one time or **GOD IS THE OWNER OF EVERYTHING... PERIOD.** another, but I can only name a few that actually live it day in and day out to its fullest meaning.

I would make the bold statement that anyone who is a Christian would trust their health to God. That's why every time we pray we think of someone in our lives that needs some kind of healing and ask God to come in and cure that person of their illness or make them 'feel better'. We believe

PARTNER WITH GOD! - PSALMS 24:1
"The earth is the Lord's and everything in it, the world, and all who live in it"

9

that God has the power to do those things. Occasionally we even pray to God and ask Him for a miracle because that's the only thing that may save a loved one's life. We have faith that He can perform miracles and, if we truly believe that, should we not obey the entire verse and trust God to guide our entire lives in everything we do and everything we have? If you are like me, you have spoken the words in the first part of the following verse, *"My power and the strength of my hands have produced this wealth for me"*, probably many times, but we must shift our focus to the last line *"...But remember the Lord your God, for it is He who gives you the ability to produce wealth."* **Deuteronomy 8:17, 18.**

The quote 'In God We Trust' has been printed on our currency since 1864 and remains there today. We have seen and heard this statement our entire lives and I believe that we have become numb to what it really means. This whole idea of trust in God can be a difficult concept to fully wrap our heads around. **God is the owner of everything.... Period.** Our jobs, our future, our friendships, our relationships, our marriages, our children, our money, our clothes, our houses, etc.; everything! This thought can be very sobering once we comprehend the true meaning of that statement. It's human nature to want to take credit for the things we have done well. We want to think that *we* have earned what we have, so we can spend it however we want.

However, God's mandate is clearly seen in **Matthew 25** – the Parable of the Talents:

14 "For it will be like a man going on a journey, who called his servants and entrusted to them his property. 15 To one he gave five talents, to another two, to another one, to each according to his ability. Then he went away. 16 He who had received the five talents went at once and traded with them, and he made five talents more. 17 So also he who had the two talents made two talents more. 18 But he who had received the one talent went and dug in the ground and hid his master's money. 19 Now after a long time the master of those servants came and settled accounts with them. 20 And he who had received the five talents came forward, bringing five talents more, saying, 'Master, you delivered to me five talents; here, I have made five talents more.' 21 His master said to him, 'Well done, good and faithful servant. You have been faithful over a little; I will set you over much. Enter into the joy of your master.' 22 And he also who had the two talents came forward, saying, 'Master, you delivered to me two talents; here, I have made two talents more.' 23 His master said to him, 'Well done, good and faithful servant. You have been faithful over a little; I will set you over much. Enter into the joy of your master.' 24 He also who had received the one talent came forward, saying, 'Master, I knew you to be a hard man, reaping where you did not sow, and gathering where you scattered no seed, [25] so I was afraid, and I went and hid your talent in the ground. Here, you have what is yours.' [26] But his master answered him, 'You wicked and slothful servant! You knew that I reap where I have not sown and gather where I scattered no seed? [27] Then you ought to have invested my money with the bankers, and at my coming I should have received what was my own with interest. [28] So take the talent from him and give it to him who has the ten talents. [29] For to everyone who has will more be given, and he will have an abundance. But from the one who has not, even what he has will be taken away. [30] And cast the worthless servant into the outer darkness. In that place there will be weeping and gnashing of teeth."

The servants in this parable were stewards of the Master's talents. I have researched the actual value of a talent in New Testament times and the overwhelming assumption is that one talent was worth '20 years of wages'. In other words, the servant that was trusted with 5 talents would be considered quite well-to-do in today's values, but even the one trusted with one talent was given much. Jesus used this parable as a way to show us that *all* we are and *all* we have comes from HIM. The unfaithful steward in this parable didn't so much waste the master's money – he took it for granted and wasted an opportunity. As a result, he was judged wicked and lazy. We are responsible for what we do for God with what we have been given, and one day we will be held accountable.

There are **3** things we must understand as 'Stewards' over our 'talents' or we will never 'Get It':

1. **Our stuff is not our stuff** - *v.14, "He entrusted <u>HIS</u> property to them."*

The story is told that after John D. Rockefeller died, someone asked his accountant 'how much money did he leave?' The accountant then replied, 'He left it all!' If life experiences don't teach us that principle, then funerals should. Solomon, the wisest man ever said, *"Naked a man comes from his mother's womb, and as he comes he so departs. He takes nothing from his labor that he can carry in his hand."* **Ecclesiastes 5:15** The Apostle Paul also wrote, *"For we brought nothing into this world, and we can take nothing out of it."* **1 Timothy 6:7**

Did you know there are an estimated 60,000 storage facilities worldwide and around 48,500 are in the United States? What does that say about our culture? It screams "I LOVE MY STUFF, and when I don't have room for my stuff, I'm willing to pay someone to store my stuff! "The self-storage industry has been one of the fastest-growing sectors of the United States commercial real estate industry over the last 40 years. It generated more than $32.7 billion dollars of revenue last year, just by storing our stuff." These facts are mind blowing to me!

Not only do we have excessive possessions but we also have excessive commitments, goals, schedules, and desires. You may have never considered yourself greedy but if you have more clothes and shoes than you wear, more furniture and dishes than you use, a fully booked schedule for work or personal life, gadgets, gizmos, and more, you may want to a take long, deep look into your life. Consider the possibility that our cluttered lives are stealing time that we should be spending with God and His word, and are leaving us with fractured family lives. The Bible says, *"Watch out! Be on your guard against all kinds of greed; a man's life does not consist in the abundance of his possessions"* **Luke 12:15**.

In today's world, it's difficult, and maybe impossible, to get away from the continuous advertisements that attack us from every angle of our lives from TV commercials, facebook, twitter, internet, shopping, mail, magazines, billboards, etc... There isn't anywhere we can go to get away from this bombardment so it's no wonder we all fall into the same materialist trap. And we want to take credit for all our material successes. But the Bible makes it very clear, time and time again, that "our stuff is not our stuff" with verses like **1 Chronicles 29:12** – *"Both riches and honor come from you and You reign over all. In your hand is power and might; in Your hand it is to make great and to give strength to all."*

2. **We are expected to be productive** - *v. 21, "His master said to him, 'Well done, good and faithful servant. You have been <u>faithful</u> over a little. Enter into the joy of your master.'"*

It's not a partnership unless two contribute. God does HIS part and WE do our part. The issue is not that God doesn't do His, it's that we don't do ours. If you are reading this book, that means God has done his part in breathing life into you and he has blessed you with your unique gifts. Now it's your turn. Time to step up and do your part.

The work ethic today, by many, is quite pathetic. We just show up, wait to be told what to do, do that task with as little effort put forth as we can, and then clock out and go home. Well let me give you some advice: don't just show up - **stand out** in your work place. Have you ever been on a job and been presented with a task and thought, "that's not my responsibility so I'm not going to do it" even though you were more than qualified to complete the task? If I'm being honest with you and myself, I have. But I have learned that my success today has come from my willingness to do what no one else wanted to do.

My mom, Ginnie, demonstrated what this really means when she worked at BellSouth Mobility. We moved to Huntsville, Alabama in 1990, and in 1992 Ginnie was looking for a job to help provide for our family. She was hired at Bellsouth as a part time receptionist who would fill in when one of the other receptionists called in sick. Because of her unparalleled work ethic, she was given a full-time job. She came in every day and went out of her way to do all she could for Bellsouth, the other employees, and the clients she came in contact with. This did not go unnoticed.

Not too long after getting the full-time position, another

job was posted and Ginnie decided to apply, and behold, she got it; and didn't stop there. She continued to work hard and ended her career at Bellsouth as the Regional Director, responsible for managing hundreds of employees along with handling all of the hiring and firing.

Did I mention Ginnie achieved all this without a college degree? Were there applicants with more experience and education for each of the positions she had on her way to the top? Yes. But they all lacked one trait - her complete dedication to doing whatever needed to be done for the company to succeed at the highest level. Ginnie lived the quote: "…the harder I work the luckier I get." This quote (and others like it) has roots all the way back to one of our founding fathers, Benjamin Franklin, and is illustrated by thousands of other extremely successful people in history. Isn't it interesting that you don't hear quotes like this from people that aren't successful? Why is that? Probably because they don't want to work 'harder', they just want to get 'paid'.

3. **We will all be held accountable -** *v.19, "After a long time the master of those servants returned and settled accounts with them."*

The master returned and he settled up. Christ will one day return. When? We are not certain. However, this is certain, one day we will die and we will stand before Him and give a thorough account of our life. How are you doing with what He has generously entrusted to you to manage on His behalf? He's looking for a partner. A trusted partner who is faithfully managing the resources they have been given. We would all do well to sow more of the dollars entrusted to us into eternal things. Wouldn't you agree?

Begin today by committing your life, your finances, and everything you have to God. By recognizing this is a spiritual issue, we begin to fully understand that we are responsible as a manager/steward of the talents and gifts God has blessed us with.

In connection with this theme, we would all do well to meditate on these words of Jesus taken from **Matthew chapter 6:21-23**

"Do not store up for yourselves treasures on earth, where moths and vermin destroy, and where thieves break in and destroy. But store up for yourselves treasures in heaven, where moths and vermin do not destroy, and where thieves do no break in and steal. For where your treasure is, there will your heart be also."

II. YOU NEED TO "PLAN" TO SUCCEED

Do you have a written financial plan? Do you think it

A PLAN IS LIKE A ROADMAP. would be helpful to do so? A plan is like a roadmap.   If you are going on a long journey, would you think it helpful to map it out first? The obvious answer is YES!! The Bible speaks highly of the necessity to plan. Plan your future, plan your finances. **Proverbs 22:3** (TLB) – *"A prudent man foresees the difficulties ahead and prepares (plans) for them; the simpleton goes blindly on and suffers the consequences."*

Proverbs 27:12, *"A prudent man sees evil and hides himself, the naive proceed and pay the penalty."*

PLAN! - PROVERBS 22:3

"A prudent man foresees the difficulties ahead and prepares (plans) for them; the simpleton goes blindly on and suffers the consequences."

Luke 14:28 - *"Suppose one of you wants to build a tower. Will he not first sit down and estimate the cost (plan) to see if he has enough money to complete it...."*

Who knows if it really happened or not, but the story is told that Albert Einstein, the famous physicist, was once traveling on a train when the conductor came down the aisle, punching the tickets of every passenger. When he came to Einstein, the bushy-haired scientist fumbled around in his vest pockets. He couldn't find his ticket, so he searched his trouser pockets. It wasn't there, so he looked in his briefcase but couldn't find it. Then he looked in the seat beside him. He still couldn't find it.

The conductor said, "Dr. Einstein, I know who you are. We all know who you are. I'm sure you bought a ticket. Don't worry about it."

Einstein nodded appreciatively. The conductor continued down the aisle punching tickets. As he was ready to move to the next car, he turned around and saw the famous man down on his hands and knees looking under his seat for his ticket.

20

The conductor rushed back and said, "Dr. Einstein, Dr. Einstein, don't worry, I know who you are. No problem. You don't need a ticket. I'm sure you bought one."

Einstein looked at him and said, "Young man, I too, know who I am. What I don't know, without my ticket, is where I'm going."

The point of the story is that traveling without a destination is pointless. Several quotes exist in the archives of literature about this. Author Lewis Carroll (*Alice in Wonderland*) is quoted as saying: "If you don't know where you are going, any road will get you there." Actually, the quote is a paraphrased rendering of a conversation between Alice and the Cheshire Cat in chapter six of Carroll's famous book.

"Would you tell me, please, which way I ought to go from here?"
"That depends a good deal on where you want to get to," said the Cat.
"I don't much care where--" said Alice.
"Then it doesn't matter which way you go," said the Cat.[5]

The most colorful quote, however, is attributed to Yogi Berra, the master of the unintentional (maybe) malapropism. There are actually two versions of this quote:

"If you don't know where you are going, you might wind up someplace else," and "You've got to be very careful if you don't know where you are going, because you might not get there."[6] Whether the famous Yankee catcher ever actually uttered either one or not, they still make the point splendidly that to get anywhere you must have a destination in mind.

As financial advisors, such a concept is a core belief for us. You never plan to fail, you just fail to plan. We are big believers that successful people – in every area of life but especially financially – are planners.

(The following story told by Pete Benson illustrates the importance of planning)

A few years ago, my wife, Ginnie, and I were invited to hold a financial conference in Velden, Austria, for a group of missionaries who had come together from their assignments all over Europe. It was a long trip from central

22

Tennessee to Austria and back, so Ginnie and I decided to make a two-week vacation out of it.

For several months, in our spare time, we went on the internet to search out various places we wanted to visit on the trip. It was daunting trying to figure out which cities and countries to select. We also tried to iron out which hotels we would stay in, but there were thousands to pick from. Then there were the little niggling details about transportation. What was the best way to get from place to place? We had no idea. There was conflicting advice on the internet and it was difficult to find unbiased information. The big pieces of the puzzle were clear to us. We wanted to spend a day or two in Paris, visit Germany and see Venice and Rome. What we couldn't put together were the details of how to do that in the most efficient manner.

We worked on it a few months ourselves, but as the time for the trip approached we were feeling less and less confident. We decided to swallow our pride and hire a professional to map it all out for us. We had no idea what a pleasant experience this would be.

When the travel agent met with us, we knew we had made the right decision. She asked us dozens of questions to get a feel for what we really wanted out of the trip and then mapped out a wonderful journey for us. She left nothing to chance. All the details were neatly buttoned up. On the last visit to the travel agent's office, before the trip, she presented us with a thick book consisting of every detail of the trip from beginning to end. We knew the times of every flight, how to get to every hotel, train station, restaurant, and village along the way. Our delightful 13-day European vacation took us through four countries without a single hitch. We were so thankful that we didn't try "winging it" the way we started. Who knows where we would have ended up had it not been for the able assistance of a fully-trained, competent, professional travel planner?

How unfortunate it is that people will spend as many as 80,000 hours working for more than 40 years and yet not spend the time necessary to map out their finances and plan for their retirement. From our vantage point as financial counselors, far too many people seem to be ambling aimlessly along, hoping and praying that everything will just turn out all right. Hope is not a plan.

All through our lives we need to be following a strategy of some kind. In our earlier years, we need to follow a budget. We must set aside an emergency fund, arrange for children's education, plan how and when we are going to buy our next car, decide when and whether we are going to purchase or rent a home.

Before the days of the GPS (Global Positioning System) we had the good, old-fashioned road map. It was unthinkable for a family to go off on a long vacation involving automobile travel to unfamiliar places without first obtaining a road map on which to mark out the route. As a matter of fact, at every gas station there was a rack of complimentary road maps, free with a fill-up. Sadly, the vast majority of Americans spend more time planning their next vacation than planning the rest of their lives in retirement.

DETERMINE VALUES AND SET GOALS

Planning starts with making some simple (often not easy, but simple) decisions and putting them down in writing.

VALUES - What are the most important things in life to you? Have you ever listed them? This is a crucial step in planning; it's like plotting your destination before a trip. These values may change over time. For example, when you are young, just starting out in life, your values may center on entertainment, obtaining nice cars, and a big home. Later it may be providing an education for your children or becoming debt-free. Still later on in life, your values may lean more in the direction of providing an income for retirement, traveling, giving money to your church or other charities, or perhaps arranging your affairs so that you are able to retire early. Whatever the case, name your top five values in order of priority and *write them down*. Why is it important to put them in writing? One reason is that the very exercise of writing them down forces you to organize them. Also, recording your values in writing sets you up nicely for the second step.

GOALS - Set your goals. If values are the destination, then goals represent the roadmap which will take you there.

Charles Shultz, creator of the cartoon strip *Peanuts*, was capable of conveying many thought-provoking ideas through the little round-headed children he drew. For example, the one I heard about where the strip's protagonist, Charlie Brown, appears in the first frame pulling back the string of a bow. The arrow is pointed slightly up. We can't see the target but we assume he is shooting at something.

In the second frame, we see Charlie Brown over by a fence where his arrow has embedded itself in the wood.

In the third frame, Charlie Brown is painting a bull's eye around the arrow.

Then Lucy comes running up in the last frame and says, "Charlie Brown, you blockhead! That's not how you do it!" To which Charlie Brown responds: "But this way, Lucy, I never miss."

Do you know anyone who operates this way concerning their finances, hoping for success with no goal in mind? Charlie Brown made no apologies for taking such a shortcut, did he? In fact, he rationalized that if he had no target he couldn't miss! When it comes to financial matters that is unfortunately how many people go through life.

The "Tyranny of the Urgent"

In the 1960s, Charles Hummel published a little booklet called *Tyranny of the Urgent*,[7] which quickly became a best seller and a business classic. In it, Hummel pointed out that there is a regular tension between things that are **urgent** and things that are **important**. Far too often, says Hummel, the urgent wins.

In the business world the urgent demands of your boss, your client, or petty office relationships, can often take priority over important things like thoroughly completing a task before starting the next one, or building unity in a work team which would instill camaraderie and longevity. The *urgent*, though less important, gets priority, while the *important* is put on the back burner. That's why it is tyrannical. While you are yielding to that urgent impulse, greasing the squeaky wheel, you are delayed from your reaching your goal.

In Charlie Brown's case, he didn't aim and then shoot; he shot and then aimed. How convenient it is to just draw a target where your arrow lands! Charlie Brown, like many people, wanted instant gratification with no effort. What is our "tyranny of the urgent?" And how do we know we are hitting the target/goal if there is no target/goal?

Do you think the church you attend has a plan? Do they have regular board meetings so they can track their progress and make sure they are 'on course'? What about the company you work for, do you think they have a business strategy? Do you think they likely meet regularly to

"I WANT TO EARN ALL I CAN, AND SAVE ALL I CAN, SO I CAN GIVE ALL THAT I CAN!"[8]

John Wesley

update and track the plan and make adjustments when necessary for ultimate success? Of course! Well, guess what? Your family is a 'business'! For my family, I call it "The Benson Family Business". What would yours be named? Think of it this way. If a young couple gets married today at age 23 and they live to age 93, then they will need enough money to survive for 70 years. Let's say for instance, their household income averaged $50,000 per year; then they have been entrusted with $3.5 million over their lifetime. If they averaged $75,000 per year it would be $5.2 million; if it was $100,000 per year it would add up to $7 million. Some of you readers will be entrusted with more than $10 million over your lifetime. Well, wouldn't you think that needs to be planned for? That's a lot of money. The reason we don't realize this is because it doesn't come to us all at once, it's spread out over many decades and comes to us in weekly, bi-weekly, or monthly allotments.

Even John Wesley had a financial plan: He said, "I want to earn all I can, and save all I can, so I can GIVE all that I can!"[8]

For a married couple that wants to develop a financial program, how do you get started? A good first step would be to commit to this undertaking. This strategy should incorporate short term (one year) financial goals; just get out a piece of paper and start jotting them down. Write whatever comes into your head. Then you need to set down several mid-term (two through five year) goals as well. What do you want to accomplish in that time period? Next, write down some longer-term goals (six through fifteen years). And lastly, record some ultra-long-term goals (fifteen through thirty years). Writing all these out is a great start (more than most families in America have ever done) and it may take several attempts to zero in on exactly what goals you really want to stick with and accomplish.

YOUR LIFE DOESN'T GET BETTER BY CHANCE, IT GETS BETTER BY CHANGE!

Next step is to designate a specific day and time when you will review, revisit, and discuss these goals and your implementation of them. Ideally this should be a set time each week; even fifteen to thirty minutes would be great. Commit to this meeting and stick to it.

The next all-important step to ensure success with your plan is to have a detailed tracking mechanism. Know your numbers (income, expense, savings, etc.) and track, track, track. It doesn't have to be a sophisticated tracking system, and in fact, simple is better, but keep good records. That way you can monitor your progress and then you get to celebrate your wins!

Lastly, I can't emphasize enough how imperative it is that you have an accountability partner to keep you on task and on plan. Accountability is key! Without it, failure is almost certain; with it, success rules the day. Who will your accountability partner be?

Your life doesn't get better by *chance*, it gets better by *change*! And that change comes by having a plan. Ok, now you are ready to plan your work, and work your plan.

III. BUDGET RULES

Financial Freedom comes from "Breaking the Law," the Parkinson Law that was developed by C. Northcote Parkinson many years ago, and he explains why most people retire poor. The law says that no matter how much money people earn, they tend to spend the entire amount. In essence, expenditures rise in lock step with your income. The more we make - the more we spend. This mentality shows that any fool can make money but it takes a wise man to know how to spend it.

How many of you have ever asked the question, "Where did my money go"? I know I have, more times than I care to admit. How can you know where it goes if you don't track it? We spend years of our lives going to school and college educating ourselves to find a job that we enjoy and that

NEED FOR A BUDGET! - PROVERBS 27:23
"Be sure you know the condition of your flocks. Give careful attention to your herds..."

provides a good financial life. Then when we get our first paycheck, it's spent before it hits our bank account. If Americans would spend 30 minutes per week planning their money, they would be happier, have more, want for less, give more, and most importantly have the confidence to take on whatever life may throw in their direction.

Imagine you have one dollar and only one chance to spend it. That's it, one time. Now, you can get another dollar bill, but you can never get that first dollar back - ever. You will either spend it or invest it. That choice will either get you *closer to* or *further from* your goals.

I believe that most of you would agree with that principle, but would also tell yourselves to "just spend it, you'll make another dollar." The problem is that immediately after spending that dollar there will be something else you want even MORE. So, you spend another dollar, and then another, and then another, until all of your dollars are gone. It's like getting on a hamster wheel without a way to get off. We just continue to dig deeper and deeper until there is no way out except bankruptcy, foreclosure, or extreme poverty.

WEALTH AND FINANCIAL FREEDOM REQUIRE SOME *TOUGH CHOICES* - EVERY DAY!

According to a recent report from CareerBuilder, nearly 78% of full-time workers said they live from paycheck to paycheck.

Wealth and financial freedom require some **tough choices** – every day! We have to learn to say NO! I have the opportunity to meet hundreds of families every year from all different walks of life and I have yet to meet one that said they don't want financial freedom; however, in reality, there are very few people that actually have it. Just as every company, big or small, has a fiscal plan for how they are going to spend their money, every family should have a similar plan. Your family is your business, and it needs a plan too. How much success your business has depends on how well you plan. Just as a business will fail if they don't have a business plan, so will your family fail if you follow the same paths. *"The plans of the diligent lead surely to abundance, but everyone who is hasty comes only to want."* **Proverbs 21:5**

Impulsive spending will lead you to empty pockets and things that will be soon outdated. Planning before you spend your money will lead to a successful family, business, giving, and rewarding purchases.

There are few feelings in life better than setting a goal and then achieving it! Reaching our goals takes dedication and discipline. Everyone wants to succeed and have financial freedom, but only a few do what it takes to have it. We have to work to earn money; it also takes work to know how to spend it. We have to create a "Spending Plan".

HAVE A BUDGET – A SPENDING PLAN!

It seems most people dislike the dreaded "B" word – but the "B" in budget doesn't stand for BAD, it stands for BARRIER. It's a matter of perception. We adore freedom and despise restraints. But remember, it is the barrier on the mountain road that restrains us from plunging over the cliffs to our  death below. Think of a budget as a protective barrier that keeps us from falling into an abyss of financial devastation. A budget is nothing more than a short range plan for how to spend money during the next six to twelve months. A budget should not restrict your freedom to enjoy life… it should expand it by helping you live within your means! John Maxwell said it best: "A budget is people telling their money where to go instead of wondering where it went."

A budget helps you decide ***how you*** are going to spend your monthly allotment/income; it is your passport to a healthy financial life. It's how you control your money instead of letting money control you. This does not mean that every month your spending will be exactly the same as the last month. Every month brings different needs and inevitably things will happen that throw you off course a little bit. But, a budget can help you anticipate these events and keep you on track with little adjustments. It keeps you in line. For example, once an airplane gets up to 10,000 feet, autopilot is engaged to navigate the rest of the flight until landing. While in route, the plane will be off-course 99% of the time due to headwinds, updrafts, downdrafts, and other weather patterns, but the autopilot gets it back on course. Our life is no different. Things happen every day to disrupt our navigation, but a Budget, or "our autopilot," will help us get to the destination.

If you are out of BAD debt (everything but primary residence) and have an adequate emergency fund (4-6 months of expenses), then your budget should look like this:

> ## 10/10/5/75 FINANCIAL BUDGET
> 10% = God First (Tithe)
> 10% = Yourself Second (Investments for Future)
> 75% = Living Expenses (Standard of Living)
> 5% = Emergency Fund
>
> **If you are out of BAD debt (everything but home) and have an adequate emergency fund (4-6 months of expenses)

For many of you reading this you may be thinking, "How in the world could I ever have a budget like the one above?" Don't worry, you are not alone. I don't expect you, immediately after reading this, to be able to change everything you are doing today and have the means to start implementing your budget like the one above. But what you need to do is get a budget written and begin following it. Over time as you begin to pay down debt, earn more from your job, and spend more wisely, you will begin to see how very possible it is to have a budget like the one above.

HAVE A TRACKING PLAN!

To achieve the financial freedom to give, save, and live within a budget, it is vital to have a tracking plan. **Proverbs 27:23** says, *"Be sure you know the condition of your flocks. Give careful attention to your herds…"*

> **"BE SURE YOU KNOW THE CONDITION OF YOUR FLOCKS. GIVE CAREFUL ATTENTION TO YOUR HERDS…"**
> Proverbs 27:23

It was 2005, and I(Dan) had just graduated from Southern Wesleyan University with my bachelor's degree. Less than one week later, I was a part of the working class. I had monthly bills and obligations that demanded a lot of my time and what little money I had. My dad came up to visit me and help me move into the townhome I was renting. While he was there, he used that time to teach me many of the skills discussed in this book. He also taught me the "little pocket notepad" exercise; he told me to carry it around in my back pocket and write down everything I bought and what it cost. He told me not to worry about keeping up with the total, just do it every day for 60 days - so I did. This exercise has forever changed my life. To this day, I perform this exercise every year or two to help me see where my money is going and what it is being spent on. Every time I do it, I find money that I'm spending on things I really don't want or need. Can I be brutally honest with you? Many of you don't want to find out where your money is going, and do you want to know why? I'll tell you: it's too painful to find out the truth. We are afraid to really know where our money is going because it forces us to face the truth about the areas in our life where we overspend carelessly. But I encourage you, do not be afraid! The Bible says, *"For God has not given us a spirit of _fear_ and timidity, but of power, love, and self discipline."* **2 Timothy 1:7** (NLT). Do this one little task and I guarantee your eyes will be opened, and you will ***find*** extra money every month.

Another relevant verse is found in **Hebrews 12:11**, *"No discipline seems pleasant at the time, but painful. Later on, however, it produces a harvest of righteousness."* Here's that great motivator, Jim Rohn again, "We must all suffer from one of two pains: the pain of discipline or the pain of regret. The difference is discipline weighs ounces while regret weighs tons."[9] Now that's good stuff!! We want the harvest of righteousness but it's not given to us. It has to be earned and it won't be easy. Don't wish it were easier, wish you were better! If you're not happy with where your finances are, do something about it!

Work harder, further your education, read more personal development books, work two jobs, spend smarter, and plan better.

I was taught as a young boy that "if it is to be, it's up to me," and I use that philosophy in all aspects of my life. The Bible states very clearly in **Proverbs 3** that we are to continue to seek wisdom all our life, and those who do will be greatly rewarded. *"Blessed are those who find wisdom, those who gain understanding, for she is more profitable than silver and yields better returns than gold. She is more precious than rubies; nothing you desire can compare with her. Long life is in her right hand; in her left hand are riches and honor. Her ways are pleasant ways, and all her paths are peace. She is a tree of life to those who take hold of her; those who hold her fast will be blessed."*

When you are finished reading this book, you'll have all the knowledge you need. However, only *'applied knowledge'* will change you. Applied knowledge is powerful. Once we have the knowledge we need, the next step is to put it action. And not tomorrow, or next week, or next month, or next year… NOW! Immediately stop what you are doing and TAKE ACTION! We have to adopt the philosophy of "If it is to be, it's up to me". Stop blaming the job you currently have, the amount of income you have, your boss that's too demanding for what little pay you get, the lack of free time you have to spend doing it, and just do it! We will make time for the things that are important to us. If planning for you and your family's financial security is not a priority, it should be. Stop being selfish; suck it up, and get to work! Take

ONLY 'APPLIED KNOWLEDGE' WILL CHANGE YOU. APPLIED KNOWLEDGE IS POWERFUL.

responsibility for where you are in life. If you're not happy with your life, change it. It is that simple!

If you need help with where to start I recommend you get on your computer, tablet, or smart phone and Google these words: "Free Budget". I have done this and there are 431 million search results, so I'm confident you can find a few good resources. However, if you don't want to aimlessly scour the internet, you can also look up Joseph Sangl or Dave Ramsey, and on their websites, you will find a plethora of resources including free budget software. A written spending plan for your money that includes giving, saving, and spending is essential to achieving financial freedom. There is nothing more powerful than planning your spending **BEFORE** any of the money ever shows up and **BEFORE** the month begins. There are NO excuses so begin today!

IV. CONTROL DEBT

Proverbs 22:7 - *"The rich rule over the poor, and the borrower is the servant to the lender."* Now answer me honestly, do you like to be ruled over? Do you like to be a servant to other people or institutions? Likely the answer is a resounding NO! Debt is mentioned quite often in

"FOR LACK OF DISCIPLINE THEY WILL DIE, LED ASTRAY BY THEIR OWN GREAT FOLLY."

Proverbs 5:23

the Bible. It may not call debt a sin but it sure doesn't look favorably on it! **Romans 13:8** says, *"Let no debt remain outstanding except the continuing debt to love one another".* Borrowing is permitted, but it is not acceptable to have past due debt. **Proverbs 5:23** says, *"For lack of discipline they will die, led astray by their own great folly."* I'm convinced that the lack of discipline in the use and abuse of credit cards has been the financial death of

DEBT! - ROMANS 13:8
"Let no debt remain outstanding except the continuing debt to love one another. Borrowing is permitted, but it is not acceptable to have past due debt."

millions of families. Warning: don't fall into the debt pit! Our advice is that if you ever carry a balance on your credit cards, cut them up immediately.

North Americans are swimming in a red sea of debt. The vast majority are drowning, or they have at least gone down for the two count. In the United States our Federal and State governments are 'fiscally irresponsible' if I must say so. It's almost to the point

where you'd say, "watch everything they do and do just the opposite!" As a country, at the time of this writing, the United States is now $20 trillion in debt. See www.usdebtclock.org. Not only are the Federal and State governments in serious debt, so are a high percentage of the citizens. According to NerdWallet: Federal Reserve debt figures as of Q3 2016, "the average mortgage debt stands at $172,806, and represents a total pool of $1.1 trillion. Student loan debt averages $49,042 by household and makes up a pool of $1.3 trillion in debt. Personal-finance website GoBankingRates recently surveyed more than 7,000 people in all 50 states and Washington, D.C., and found that "paying off debt," (i.e. credit cards) was the main financial stressor for those in 32 states, including New York, Florida, and California. The second-most common response was not having enough money to fund an emergency, the main stress for those in Arizona, South Dakota, Wisconsin, Missouri, Oklahoma, Arkansas, Mississippi and Connecticut. In 2016, according to the American Bankruptcy Institute, there were 770,846 personal bankruptcies. That's a large number! However, there have been many years in the last decade that in excess of 1 million families declared bankruptcy. Now, it's a fact that some of those could not be avoided and were not brought on by reckless and over spending. But it's also a fact that a high percentage were caused by "easy money," abuse of credit cards, reckless spending, no financial education, and living beyond one's means. It's my opinion that having no personal debt is a goal to shoot for and can be attained by ordinary citizens like you and me. At least getting to the place where the only debt is your home mortgage is attainable if people will just be disciplined and follow the principles in this book. Though it's certainly not guaranteed, you stand a good likelihood that your primary residence will increase in value over time. Even with the purchase of your home, you need to set a realistic budget and stick to it. Do not let anyone talk you into buying more than you need or can afford. It's just not smart and likely won't end well for you.

What's really bad is going into debt for a depreciating asset. Yet, millions of families do that every year. So then, you say, "what is BAD debt?" Bad debt is things like automobiles, furniture, vacations, clothes, jewelry, entertainment, etc.... These all depreciate in value over time.

Many of the problems we incur with debt in our lives is because we have made bad choices. Not always, but very often. And on the other hand, if you are debt free, it's also because of *good* choices you have made. In fact, life is about choices. For more on the subject of choices, I recommend reading the book written by Darren Hardy, "The Compound Effect". In this book, he teaches that your life today is the compound effect of all the choices you have made throughout your life. You have choices, and I have choices. And few if any of you will make the choices I made and make. I can tell you, I chose early on that I would be a person who would 'pay as I go' and *if I couldn't pay, I wouldn't have.* Other than a couple of pieces of real estate, if I can't pay cash, I don't buy. I don't borrow. You say that's easy, you make good money, you can afford to. Oh really, allow me the personal privilege to tell you the real story.

The year is 1984, I'm 25 years old, married with three children and I have just moved my family of five to Prince Edward Island, Canada, to pioneer a brand-new church, Island Wesleyan Church. Our only family income was what we were paid by the Wesleyan Church as church planters in this community. I can assure you we were not making big money. I believe it was around $20,000 annually, and we needed a car. This would be our only car, but we did need at least one for transportation of our family to get to work, school, and church. So, I did what everyone does. I went to the bank to inquire about getting a loan. I left the bank loan officer with papers in hand giving me the information on securing my loan. Upon arriving home and reading the loan papers in detail it came to light that we would be borrowing $2500 but because of interest, we would actually be paying $3200 in total. So, let me get this straight, I'm going to buy a car for $2500 that is likely worth less than $2000, then I'm going to over-pay for it because I have to pay the bank an additional $700 on top of all that - just for the privilege of borrowing the money. That just did not sit well with me, but we really needed a car. So, I looked in our bank accounts and the little bit we had saved and decided that we could afford to buy a car for cash, as long as we didn't pay more than $800.00. After praying, looking around, and talking to folks in our church and community we found the car. Have you ever heard of a 'DUCK' car? Perhaps it was a brand before all you were born. Actually,

 it was a 1972 AMC Hornet, four-door, with an orange body and white roof. Power steering? You bet, all the power you could muster. Our two daughters, Ginger and Amanda, nick-named it the 'Duck' car because when we would drive them to school they would yell to each other, "Duck!" They were embarrassed for their friends to see them in it. Depreciation, well we didn't really have to worry about that. I mean, how much more could the value drop? Now don't get me wrong, I qualified to get a loan at a bank and get a 'real' car, but I made a choice; a choice not to do what's expected, or normal. That's where I'm different than most people. And it gets better. Though I'm no mechanic, (and that's a huge understatement) we prayed over, duct taped, and cheered that car on for two strong years. Yes, we got two years running out of that beauty. And

guess what else we did? During that 24 months, we paid ourselves a car payment equal to the payment we would have paid had we taken the loan from that bank. So, when the Duck car died and was buried, we had saved up over $2400 towards the next vehicle purchase. On top of that, in the mid 1980's banks actually paid interest on your money deposited in the bank, and over that 24 months we had earned an additional $350 in interest; so, we now had $2750 in cash to go buy our next vehicle. And that's how it began. Since then, I have always paid cash for cars. I don't know what it's like to take out a loan for a car. We simply buy the car in cash, then pay ourselves a monthly car payment in a separate account and then we have the funds to buy the next car when we need it. I know I'm weird, right? But I've kind of grown fond of weird. I like being free. Free from the debt shackles that bind. Now, how many of you would like to pay cash for cars? My bet is that all of you would. Well, guess what, you can! If I can do it, you certainly can. Remember, it's more about discipline than it is about dollars. There's one more thing to add: in addition to the discipline, you also have to be willing to swallow your pride. When you know you can buy a much nicer car by getting a loan, but you buy a lesser car with cash, your pride takes a bruising.

Sometimes the pathway to being debt free is creativity, and many times it's about grit, hard work and sacrifice. Pardon the personal examples but I'm going to tell you another interesting story. In late August of 1977, at the age of 18, I put a few pieces of old, ugly, used, and broken furniture, a few packed suitcases, my wife (age 18), and our daughter Ginger (age 9 months) into a borrowed pickup truck. We moved to Sussex, New Brunswick, Canada so I could attend Bethany Bible College (now known as Kingswood University) beginning in early September. At the time, we had maybe $300.00 in our bank account, and we moved into a very small apartment. I didn't have college funding. I didn't have any scholarships, and I didn't have a job (sounds like I also didn't have a brain). Additionally, there are several things you need to know about me. I'm not good with electronics, I know nothing about mechanics/cars, I'm allergic to dust, and I was never made to clean at the home I grew up in. So, I started looking for a job. The first job I landed was in the electronics department of a large department store. (Wow, God sure has a sense of humor.) However, one job was not going to cut it. I needed several jobs. I also landed a job out at the ESSO gas station on the Trans Canada Highway, pumping gas, checking oil, and tire pressure. The college also gave me a few hours of work each week vacuuming floors, cleaning toilets, and doing other general cleaning. As a bonus, every now and then I was asked to go out to the pulp and paper mill, and from midnight to 4:00 a.m., we would clean the machines of all the sawdust. I especially liked this job because the pay was much greater than the other jobs. Thinking back though, at least two times I was sent to the emergency room at the hospital with an asthma attack. However, those jobs sure helped pay for some baby food and college bills. I'm serious, you can't make this stuff up.

God found me jobs alright; in electronics, with cars, cleaning toilets, and in a dust storm. I'll tell you what else God, Ginnie, and I did—we left that college four years later having never missed a  meal, never missed a bill payment, and not owing the college (or anyone else for that matter) one RED cent! We were debt free! We serve an amazing God and one who is *"able to do immeasurably more than we could ever ask and imagine"* **Ephesians 3:20.**

I tell you that not to boast at all, but to give you hope! This kind of thing is doable for ordinary people willing to do extraordinary things. Napolean Hill, author of the book, Think and Grow Rich, once said, "the man who does more than he is paid for, will soon be paid for more than he does."[10] I also like the quote by Saint Augustine, **"Pray** as if everything depends on God, and **work** as if everything depends on man."[11] Another quote I've heard from John Maxwell that fits well here: "You can *pay* now and *play* later OR you can *play* now and *pay* later. Either way, you have to pay."[12]

1. How did we get IN this mess?

Answer: A screwed up mindset! Others have it so why shouldn't I, and why should I wait, when I don't have to? John D. Rockefeller was once asked, "How much money is enough?" He quickly replied, "Just a little bit more". We live in a very materialistic society. We have this insatiable hunger to keep up with and even get ahead of our neighbors. It's like some kind of an endless competition - "keeping up with the Jones." So, we end up spending money we don't have on things we don't really need to impress people who frankly don't even care. How does that make sense? Will Rogers once said, "we'll show the world we are prosperous, even if we have to go broke to do it." Here's

> **"MONEY FLOWS EFFORTLESSLY TO THAT WHICH IS YOUR HEART'S GREATEST LOVE."**[13]
> Tim Keller

how – Buy NOW…. Pay FOREVER!!!!! And do it all on our Perpetual Payments Credit Card. Research shows that there are several billion new credit card solicitations sent out to Americans each and every year. Have you also noticed that nearly every retailer wants you to sign up for their credit card? Why wait when it's so easy to just CHARGE IT? Don't fall for it. It's a deadly trap. But, we want it all and we want it now. How about we exercise a rare trait known as delayed gratification? Many of the things we call needs are actually just wants. Tim Keller once said, "money flows effortlessly to that which is your heart's greatest love."[13]

Think about this one for a good while; debt is one of the few things you can own at no cost. So, you may be asking right now, should I have a credit card at all? Here's my answer: do you ever carry a balance? If so, then I would say

NO, you shouldn't have a credit card. Use a debit card, or cash. That way you have to actually have the money before you spend it or buy something. If you can go 2 years or more and you have not carried a balance, AND you have a generous portion saved up in an emergency fund, and your plan is to pay off your balance every month, you should be OK to have a credit card. But keep in mind you don't need more than one or two. Shred the rest. Now!

2. HOW DO WE GET OUT OF THIS MESS?

Let me say this very clearly: It's a lot harder to get out of this mess than it was to get into this mess. The first thing you need to do is stop the bleeding. Cut up some cards and stop making it easy to add to the problem. Secondly, you need to realize that there is hope and you can do this. Next you need to put together a strict budget for your current and future spending, and make sure you implement a tracking mechanism. Also, be certain all adults in the household are on board with the strategy and goals. After you have taken these steps, you need to begin a program to pay off current debts. If possible, begin with the lowest balances and pay those off quickly to get some wins under your belt. Victories motivate you on towards your goals. Move onto the next debt, and so on and so on. And remember, don't add to the debt.

If you don't have a viable emergency fund built up, you have to get working on that also. Set up a separate fund just for emergencies. You must get that funded as quickly as you can. Otherwise, your credit card becomes your emergency fund. Now you have a no-win vicious cycle. Ideally your emergency fund will get built up to several months expenses. Even a few hundred or a few thousand dollars is a good beginning. You say, "But Pete, this is just not normal; this living below your means, having a strict budget and cutting up credit cards." Well let Pete tell you what 'normal' is: NORMAL has 8 credit cards, is $15,000 in debt on those cards, is paying 15-20% interest on those cards, has no emergency fund, no money saved for college for children, very little put aside for retirement, has inadequate life insurance, and is a handful of paychecks from bankruptcy, has several ulcers and doesn't sleep well at night! That's what normal is! But normal also eats out 3-4 times per week. Lives in a home larger than they can afford, drives a car that is newer and more expensive than they should have, has iphones, Apple computers, big screen TV's and even borrows to buy furniture and take vacations. It's no wonder

Dave Ramsey says, "normal is broke".

Now if you take all the steps listed above, and you are still making slow progress, perhaps you need to begin selling some things. Take the proceeds from those sales and apply that to the debt. You may also need to get a second or third job. There are two ways to have more money: *spend less* and *earn more*. I know a professional executive who swallowed his pride and delivered pizzas 3 nights a week to help supplement his goals to get out of debt quickly. That was a big bruise to his ego, but desperate times call for desperate measures. Does someone you know need to hire to have their grass cut, dogs walked, cars washed, snow shoveled, or house cleaned? You get the picture. Be creative, and be determined.

V. CREATE AN EMERGENCY FUND

If I gave you the choice between being a "wise man" or a "foolish man", which would you choose? Would you even really have to think about the answer? If you do then we already know you're the foolish man. Of course, we all want to be wise. Well the Bible gives us instructions on how to be a wise man with not only our actions but also our money. **Proverbs 21:20**

IT'S ESTIMATED THAT OVER 66 MILLION AMERICANS HAVE NOTHING, THAT'S RIGHT NOTHING, ZERO, ZILCH, NOTTA SET ASIDE FOR EMERGENCIES.

states, *"The wise man saves for the future, but the foolish man spends whatever he gets..."* It's as simple as that. If you want to be wise with your money you need to save for the future.

So, let me ask the question another way, "Do you want

SAVING! - PROVERBS 21:20
"The wise man saves for the future, but the foolish man spends whatever he gets..."

to be like the wise man who saves for the future and financial emergencies which are unknown… or like the foolish man that spends every dime he gets and risks losing everything during financial hardships?" Again, everyone would say that they want to be like the wise man but unfortunately, statistics show that we're not practicing it. The numbers speak for themselves. It's estimated that over 66 million Americans have nothing, that's right nothing, zero, zilch, notta set aside for emergencies. Currently, 47 percent of Americans say they could not afford an emergency expense of $400, or would cover it by selling something or borrowing money, according to a separate report by the Federal Reserve Board's Division of Consumer and Community Affairs.

What does this mean? Well it means that most of your friends, neighbors, and family members have to rely on using a credit card for their next emergency. If we don't have the money for it today, we probably won't have it tomorrow and so it begins a never-ending snowball of debt that is sure to end in disaster.

As stated earlier, the U.S. government is a great example of *how not to run your personal household* (the Canadian government is not much better, and the Eurozone is in a world of hurt). The U.S. is trillions of dollars in debt, then they go to war where the cost is beyond description, then the unexpected emergencies hit, not once, not twice, but again

and again. Fortunately for them, they have a printing press downstairs and so they just keep printing more and more money. But eventually we have to pay the piper. You may not be in the type of debt mentioned above but most of you are just one emergency away from total despair, bankruptcy, repossession, and way beyond the point of just being broke.

There's a book by Richard A Swenson, *"MARGIN: Restoring Emotional, Physical, Financial, and Time Resources, to Overloaded Lives"* in which there are many great strategies we could all benefit from. But for our purposes, he uses this analogy for 'Margin' in finances – Think of a full glass of water, one more drop breaks the dam and causes overflow. There needs to be room in the glass!

In case you haven't realized this already, I'll let you in on an extremely valuable secret... Wait for it... Are you ready?..... *unexpected financial emergencies happen*, and they don't happen at "good times". I know this is shocking to many of you but it's true. There is never a good time to get hit with a financial emergency or unexpected costs. It just doesn't have to negatively impact your day to day finances, or family, or marriage if you've planned for it in advance.

You have to be disciplined, stick to your budget and savings plan, put money away consistently like clockwork, and don't stray. Your emergency fund has to be in a separate account apart from your normal account that's used for your daily living expenses and it needs to be easily and quickly accessible.

The main objective of the emergency fund is to be able to tackle any financial crisis we are dealt, no matter how big or how small. But it also has one more significant built-in bonus; it relieves stress, and gives us peace of mind. You'll immediately feel the weight lifted off your shoulders knowing you no longer have to worry about small financial emergencies. And once you get your larger emergency fund established you won't have to worry about most of the big ones either.

Your goal is to accumulate 4-6 months living expenses in your emergency fund. This is not to be confused with income but rather expenditures you have to pay every month to survive. For many of you this may seem like an impossibly daunting task. But every one of you 'can' do this. Start somewhere, no matter how small. Try to get to $100, then to $500, then to $1000, then try to get to one month's expenses, and once you get there try for 3 months, and so on. I believe in your ability to accomplish this, but I'm less concerned about when you achieve your emergency fund than when you start it. The key is to just 'start', no matter how small, **start**. Remember that the journey of one thousand miles begins with a single step.

VI. INVEST FOR THE FUTURE

The previous chapters have dealt with the day-to-day financial aspects of our lives. Now we turn to our future years.

You can't afford to consume all your money and income, and you can't give it all away; you're going to need a significant amount built up for the future. That's very Biblical! And guess what? Life's biggest expense could be "RETIREMENT". For many of you, the retirement years could last 20-30 years. That's a long, long time. For some of you, that could be almost as long as your working years. In fact, in my business, I have several clients who have now been retired longer than they worked. You must save for the future, and time is of the essence! David Chilton in his book, "The Wealthy Barbor", says, "The best time to plant

---

INVESTING! - PROVERBS 21:20

"The wise man saves for the future... In the house of the wise are stores of food and oil, but a foolish man devours all he has."

an oak tree is 20 years ago, the next best time is NOW!"[14] **Proverbs 21:20**, *"The wise man saves for the future…"* Now, it is a fact that rate of return, the profit on an investment over a period of time, plays a part in the overall growth of your money for retirement, but nothing seems to build money like time. Therefore, the sooner you get started the better. The average U.S. household is significantly behind; and not just a little behind, a long ways behind. **Proverbs 21:20**, *"In the house of the wise are stores of food and oil, but a foolish man devours all he has."*

THERE ARE 3 DYNAMICS INVOLVED IN THE CREATION OF WEALTH/RETIREMENT FUNDS:

1. How much money will you save/invest monthly and yearly?

2. What will your rate of return be on your money?

3. How many years will your money have to grow and compound?

Einstein said, "Compound interest is the 8th wonder of the world; those who understand it, earn it, and those who don't, pay it!"[15] In Darren Hardy's book, "The Compound Effect", he gives the following amazing story. He says, "If you were given a choice between taking $3 million in cash this very instant and

"COMPOUND INTEREST IS THE 8TH WONDER OF THE WORLD; THOSE WHO UNDERSTAND IT, EARN IT, AND THOSE WHO DON'T, PAY IT!"[15] Einstein

a single penny that doubles in value every day for 31 days, which would you choose? Let's say you take the cold hard cash and your friend goes with the penny route. On day five, your friend has sixteen cents. You however, have $3 million. On day ten, it's $5.12 versus your big bucks. How do you think your friend is feeling about their decision? You're probably spending your millions, enjoying the heck out of it, and loving your choice. After 20 full days, with only 11 days left, Penny Lane has only $5,243. How is she feeling about herself at this point? For all her sacrifice and positive behavior, she has barely more than $5,000. You, however, have $3 million. That's when the invisible magic of the Compound Effect starts to become visible. The same small mathematical growth improvement each day makes the compounded penny worth $10,737,418.24 on day thirty-one, more than three times your $3 million. Very few things are as impressive as the magic of compounding pennies."[16]

Let's break up this section into three age categories: the beginning stage is age 20 to age 50; middle stage is age 50 to age 65; and the last stage is age 65+ and would be the retirement stage.

1. THE BEGINNING STAGE: AGES 20-50

For young people just beginning their work career, investing for retirement just seems so far away and is therefore not a priority for many. Yet to get into the habit of long term investing, you need to open an individual retirement account (IRA) of some type and begin contributing to it with every paycheck, even if it's only 2% or 3% of your income. Just $100 per month adds up to $1200 in a year. It's a start. The goal is to work up to 10% or more, but begin with something and start building on that. Do anything at all at first and make sure you get it set up as an automatic contribution from your paycheck each pay period. For more on this topic read David Bach's book called "The Automatic Millionaire". Mr. Bach endorses this whole idea of setting up systematic contributions to your long-term retirement and has great practical advice.

Another thing to keep in mind is what type of an account to open. There are several options, however I recommend a Roth IRA account. You get no tax break now on your money going into it, but over a long period of time your money grows tax free and after age 59.5 you can withdraw all the funds (what you put into it and also what it earned) 100% tax free. Yeah! Tax-free, those are sweet words right there. Not only is the seed money pulled out tax-free but also the harvest (what it grows to). That's a good deal. Keep in mind also that at the time of this writing, anyone under age 50 can contribute up to $5500 each year. If married, then both spouses can contribute that amount so combined it is up to $11,000 annually. One more thing to consider, if retirement is a long way off, perhaps 20, 30 or even 40 years, then you need to be quite aggressive in your investment choices. See a qualified advisor for help with this, but something with low fees and a great ten-year track record for growth is optimal for this age group. Another thing I need to mention is that if your employer is offering a 401K plan or a 403B plan or some other retirement account, please look into that. Especially if the employer is matching your contributions in some capacity, perhaps 2%, 3%, or even 5% then take advantage of that. There are not many things better than free money. Your employer is offering to be a partner in your future retirement. That's something indeed to consider.

2. MIDDLE STAGE: AGES 50-65

It's always a bit difficult to give 'general' advice to families because everyone's situation can be unique, so again I recommend that you find and engage a qualified advisor to assist in a more customized plan for you. Generally, however, as we enter into this pre-retirement stage, sometimes referred to as the retirement red-zone, you begin to lower the risk a bit on your overall investments. You still likely need to be moderately aggressive up until the last 5 working years but perhaps not as aggressive as when you were 20 years younger. During this period, you likely could benefit from more asset class diversification strategies. Asset class diversification is not just standard diversification across stock market funds, it is diversification among various asset classes like: the stock market, real estate or real estate funds, bonds, alternative investments, insurance products, and so on. You certainly still need good growth on your money but you should now have a nest egg to protect and in the near future perhaps draw income from, so it's a little more hands-on at this stage. Also, keep in mind that as retirement is drawing closer, you need to develop a well thought out and specific retirement and future income plan. You could likely benefit significantly from a Retirement and Income specialist.

It's during this stage that you now need to get very serious about your investments and about retirement. In the United States, as things stand currently, once you reach age 50 you can do catch-up contributions to your IRA's, Roth IRA's, employer retirement accounts like 401K's, etc. For many middle-aged workers, they now can add a lot more to their investments, as in some cases their children are finished with college, or have gotten married and are now for the most part on their own financially. That frees up extra funds to invest for retirement. Plus, it can allow you to pay down debt which is also very important. It's not all about what you have saved for your retirement, it's also about what extra debts or bills you are carrying into your retirement golden years. In the red-zone, you need to look at developing a future income plan for those "permanent unemployment" years and as well, it's a great time to reassess your insurance needs.

It's during this stage of life that you want to re-evaluate your life insurance. It could be that in your situation you need to drop your coverage amount somewhat, while other families may even need to increase it. Always keep in mind that life insurance is a situational product and you can outlive the need for it. There are certain kinds of life insurance that generate future tax-free income that you may want to look into at this age.

Still another planning aspect to consider and seriously look into is long term care protection. More detailed information on this subject coming your way in the next chapter.

3. RETIREMENT STAGE: 65+ YEARS OLD

Once you have reached the retirement years you should have already grown your investments. Now that you have them, it's most important to keep them. So, in my opinion, this is the time of life to protect your money, and draw income from it. Growth, then, at this stage, comes in as less of a priority for many families. The same investments that get you to retirement are not the ones to get you through retirement. Some funds and accounts are best for long-term growth, and others are for income and security. For most families, the money in investments is not down the road money, it's now money. Unless you have a limitless nest-egg, you need to concentrate on protecting and keeping it. It's time to be conservative and moderate in your risk tolerance. This is the time to look into things like income funds, bonds, bank notes, fixed indexed annuities, fixed annuities, dividend paying stocks and exchange traded funds and low cost mutual funds, REITs (real estate investment trusts), interval funds that pay nice income and dividends, that sort of thing. You may not need or want all of those, but talk to a Retirement and Income specialist, take your time gathering the information, and only invest when you feel comfortable. More on selecting the right financial advisor and coach can be found in Chapter IX.

Remember not to put all your eggs in one basket. Keep in mind your time horizon for gaining losses back has changed; you may not be in the accumulation stage anymore but in the de-accumulation stage. Have you ever heard of the "Rule of 100"? It's not for everybody, but it goes like this: You subtract your age from 100 and then whatever the difference is would be the percentage to safely have at risk. For a 70-year-old they would take 100-70=30 so for them they would have no more than 30% in something where it is higher growth oriented and would have much greater risk of losing. On the other hand, someone 30 years old would most likely want to have at least 70% of their monies in high growth oriented funds. It's just a general rule of thumb but certainly something to consider as a guide.

VII. PROTECT YOUR ASSETS

If you take the steps mentioned in this book you will absolutely, without a shadow of a doubt, build assets and the value of your estate, otherwise known as your net worth. While the goal is to eventually build up your assets, once you have done that, your work is still not complete. Building assets is one thing, protecting them and providing for them is equally important.

Being a faithful, God-honoring steward involves doing proper estate planning. It can't be made any clearer than in

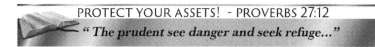

PROTECT YOUR ASSETS! - PROVERBS 27:12
" The prudent see danger and seek refuge..."

I Timothy 5:8 when it states, *"If anyone does not provide for his relatives, and especially his immediate family, he has denied the faith." The word 'provide' in this verse can simply mean to make preparation to meet a need."*

When there are things we love and hold near to our heart, we will protect them at all costs. The ones that come to mind first are, wife or husband, children, home, health, vehicles, and our ability to earn income. We can protect some of these things physically but it is equally or even more important to protect them financially as well, and I'm going to give you the <u>BIG THREE</u> to start your journey to Protection.

INSURANCE

How many of you like to pay for insurance each month? Anyone want to buy more? Many of you may feel "insurance poor" but in the end, it is critical that we properly insure the things we love and need. I certainly don't want you to pay for un-needed insurance, but I do want you to understand the important role insurance plays in our lives. The reality of insurance is that no one likes it until they need it. Let me give you an example that hits home for my family:

It was 31 years ago and my Aunt Joanne (Pete's sister) and Uncle Arthur were due to have their first baby. Joanne was 19 years old and Arthur was 24. Arthur was a lobster fisherman who worked many hours, days, nights, and even stayed out fishing on the boat for days at a time. They lived on a small island called Grand Manan (in New Brunswick, Canada) with only 2600 residents. The hospital there is a good hospital for such a small population but because certain things can go wrong with pregnancies and because there are no emergency facilities nearby, the doctors encourage the ladies when they get two to three weeks from their delivery date to stay on the mainland with relatives or a friend so they can to be near a larger hospital; Aunt Joanne did this.

The day came that Joanne was in labor. Arthur, who had been out fishing all night, got the call around 2:30 A.M. to come to the hospital. He sailed his boat to Blacks Harbour, which would have taken 3-4 hours, and jumped in a truck to drive the additional hour to the Saint John Regional Hospital. However, when he was less than 10 miles from the hospital he fell asleep at the wheel, the truck went over a bridge into a river and he was drowned; he died at the same time he was becoming a new father.

My grandfather was the first to get the news. He had to go into the hospital room where his daughter held his newborn grandson, and give her the devastating news her husband had died. Joanne now found herself a 19-year-old brand-new mother with no job because Arthur was the bread winner; she was in a real predicament.

But two months prior, Arthur had called an insurance agent and bought a life insurance policy for himself and Joanne. The agent had received the first premium but had not even had time to deliver the policy before Arthur died. My great uncle called the insurance company and began to track down the policy. He found out that the policy had been approved, and my aunt was to receive two hundred thousand dollars. Now keep in mind this was 31 years ago and at that time the average income was $37,500/year. The insurance money allowed Aunt Joanne the time that was necessary to regroup, rebuild, and land on her feet financially. Life was going to be difficult enough, but without financial pressures, it would be more tolerable.

Unfortunately, there are millions of stories just like this. In fact, LIMRA (Life Insurance Marketing and Research

Association) did a poll to see how many lower income ($50k/year income or less) and middle class (income between $50k-$250k/year) individuals died each year without life insurance. I will spare you the gory details and sum it up for you nice and neat; here are the results of the poll: 48% of the people that die each year have NO life insurance. Of the 52% that have insurance, 21% of them admitted they were underinsured. That means only 31% of people that die have proper insurance.

What these statistics really mean is that 69% of families out there will suffer financial hardship due to lack of

adequate insurance. I know this news doesn't give us the warm and fuzzies but let me give you some news that should... insurance has never been cheaper than right now.

Not long ago the insurance companies increased the longevity tables, meaning they finally admitted that people are living longer. This immediately decreased the cost for new policies being written. So now you know you do have options, and in the insurance world there are many. Take your time, find an agent that is independent, and have them shop various companies for the most competitive rate, giving you the right amount of coverage for the least annual cost.

POWER OF ATTORNEY/WILL/TRUST

How many of you feel like you have worked hard for what you have? What if I told you that 95% of you have unwanted heirs that are going to get some of what you leave behind? Would you want to know who they are? Would you disinherit them if you could? Don't worry, I'm not going leave you hanging... here they are: The Government, Probate Attorneys, Court System, and possibly even strangers. If you did not plan to leave money to any of these uninvited beneficiaries, you can change that today. There are some vital pieces to your estate plan that you need to get nailed down to ensure you have properly provided for the ones you leave behind. This is not the most exciting part of the work that needs to be done but do not procrastinate or miss any of these important documents.

A Healthcare Power of Attorney is a document that will state who will be in charge of making medical decisions for you if you are unable to do so yourself. This includes decisions to give, withhold, or withdraw informed consent to any type of health care need including, medical and surgical treatments. Other decisions that may be included are psychiatric treatment, nursing care, hospitalization, treatment in a nursing home, and home health care. I definitely don't want doctors to be the only voice as to what procedure or what kind of care I am going to get. When it comes to my health I want to be sure MY wishes are being honored and the only way to do that is to assign to someone I trust the power to make these decisions for me.

A Durable Power of Attorney is a document that allows an individual to assist with your financial matters if you become incapacitated or are unable to manage them yourself. This includes paying your mortgage, keeping bills current, paying for care, buying groceries, reviewing bank account balances to be sure you don't overdraft due to lack of funds, canceling a service that you no longer need or require, etc... the list goes on and on. Have you have ever tried to call a company and ask them questions about an account but you were not named on that account? If you have, you know and understand why this power of attorney is important. They will not talk to you, period. No if's, and's, or buts. You have no right to the information on that account, even if you are trying to help. Having a simple Durable Power of Attorney will eliminate this stress for you and your loved ones.

A living will takes care of your wishes when you become terminally ill. This document will give directives to your loved ones and doctors what type of quality of life you wish to have when you are at the end of your life. For example, whether you want feeding tubes, what type of pain relief you wish, if you want to be resuscitated or not if you are unconscious, etc. Do not leave these decisions to your loved ones to make for you; sit down and take the necessary time to make them for yourself. I have personally met with many families after this type of decision had to be made because there were no instructions left and believe me when I tell you that you do not want to put that kind of weight on anyone, not even your worst enemy. This can literally mean having to make a judgment about when someone dies and that is not something someone else should have to decide for you.

The last document needed for your estate is either a will or a trust. Jane Bryant Quinn said, "You own stuff, you will die, someone will get that stuff."[17] A will or trust states who you want to get your "stuff". Everyone has an estate plan. Even if you don't have either one of these documents in place yet, you have decided to allow the state to distribute your stuff to whom they believe it should go to. Not only can this be very expensive and time consuming, it's also a total disregard for what God has blessed you with. Don't let this be your legacy.

There are a few main differences between a will and a trust:

A will is designed to go through probate or the court system at your death. This will involve attorney fees, court costs, and time spent waiting for probate to end. While probate is not always a terrible thing, in some states it can still be costly and long, and your will can be contested by people left out of the will or those that think they deserve more than they received.

A trust is specifically designed to bypass probate and keep the estate out of the courts. There does not need to be an attorney to help settle the estate like a will requires. It is also a legally binding document that is usually not as easily contested by family members or other people if there are disagreements about who gets what. A trust is also private. A will on the other hand is public record for anyone to view.

There are many other features to consider between a will and a trust but the bottom line is you need one of them, and you need it YESTERDAY! Not having a proper estate plan is like being the steward that buried his talents. You work too hard to acquire and build an estate while you're alive; be sure to also have a plan for it when you die.

DISABILITY/LONG TERM CARE

I know, I can hear your enthusiasm as we work our way into more insurance talks. But I think you would agree that we all insure the things we can't readily write a check to replace: our home, cars, life, health, income, and more.

Disability Insurance is designed to insure your income. So, let me ask you a few questions about your income. What if your last paycheck was your last paycheck? What would the consequences be? How would you pay for your everyday expenses such as mortgage, electricity, car, gas, food, and other insurance coverages (health, auto, home, life) without your next payday? Not going to happen to you though, right? While you think about the answers to my questions above, let these statistics sink in as well:

1. Most Americans are better prepared financially to die than to become disabled, although the chances are at least three to five times greater of a disability occurring. (Source: www.mdrt.org)

2. Social Security Disability Insurance is available to people of all incomes, but only if they have worked at least 10 years before becoming disabled. The Social Security Disability Insurance program pays an average of $722 per month (considerably below the poverty level), and the disability criteria is so strict that only about 35 percent of applicants are approved. (Source: www.mdrt.org)

3. Nearly half (46 percent) of all foreclosures on conventional mortgages are caused by a disability, vs. only 2 percent that are caused by the homeowner's death. (Source: www.mdrt.org)

4. If you think this only happens to older people, think again! The sobering fact for 20-year-olds, insured for disability benefits, is that more than 1-in-4 of them becomes disabled before reaching retirement age.

(Source: www.ssa.gov)

5. A 35-year-old has a 50 percent chance of becoming disabled for a 90-day period or longer before age 65. About 30 percent of Americans ages 35-65 will suffer a disability lasting at least 90 days during their working careers. About one in seven people ages 35-65 can expect to become disabled for five years or longer. (Source: www.mdrt.org)

Don't worry, I'll spare you all the other gory details on disability. If the above statements don't wake you up, you are on a sure path to disaster. Getting proper disability coverage is not expensive when considering the alternative and can save you and your family from severe consequences when hit with a disability. And counting on Social Security to cover those expenses while you recover is not a viable option either.

What if you have already made it through your working years, are you out of harms' way? Possibly the need for disability insurance has diminished but guess what? Lucky you, you just entered into what can be the most devastating expense there is, Long Term Care. I know, I know, the news just keeps getting better. (I am now realizing why my father gave me this chapter to write).

Let me ask you a question. Let's say you just walked into retirement, have no debt, and the house you have is worth $350,000 and paid for. Now let's assume you have saved up around $500,000 in investment accounts. Would you call and cancel your homeowner's insurance? No? Why not? You have the money to rebuild it if a disaster tore the home apart. No big deal right; just write the check... Now you're all thinking I'm crazy for thinking that way and you're correct. I do not recommend you cancel your homeowner's insurance, even if you can pay to rebuild a new home or cover other potential future expenses. But if I'm crazy for thinking that way, would you be considered equally as crazy for not insuring your long-term care needs? The statistics say there's less than 1 in 3000 chance you will lose a house to a natural disaster but there is a 7 out of 10 chance you will need long term care assistance. With an average price tag of $85,000 per year for care and an average stay of 3 years, I believe this is a potential threat worth covering.

You can literally do "everything right" when it comes to saving and planning for income in retirement and miss this one little piece of the plan. If you do, it can all come tumbling down. I have a client whose wife was diagnosed with Alzheimer's at a relatively young age, in her mid 60's. She was very healthy and in fact was a former Miss Universe contestant. She has now been in a nursing home for 7 years. I met with her husband recently and asked him how she was doing and he told me that she was healthier than he was, just not mentally, and that it was possible she would out-live him. The annual cost for her care is $98,000/year. You can see how this expense could erode an estate quickly. Thankfully for them he did get a long-term care policy that has been covering the majority of the cost for her care. While I admit this real life example may be the exception and not the norm, it is a reality for their family.

Fortunately, this is an asset class that has continued to evolve and in your favor as a consumer. In years past there used to be very few options for individuals considering long term care coverage; you had to be in good health, and if you didn't use the coverage there were no benefits paid to your heirs/estate. Now there are many different options. Not all of them require health examinations to obtain coverage, and any portion not used will be left to your heirs/estate. There is literally an option for almost anyone out there that has at least saved a little money for their retirement.

Unfortunately, most people don't take the need for disability insurance and long-term care insurance seriously until it's too late. If you are already in a situation that requires this type of care, you've missed the boat.

In conclusion, you can see that there are many things to consider when it comes to protecting your assets. The good news is that help is easy to find. If you need recommendations or referrals of people that can help with this, you can talk to your church leaders, your successful friends, neighbors, your boss, etc. Take the time necessary and talk to a professional who can provide you with the answers and resources needed to protect the things you've worked hard for and love.

VIII. LEAVE A LEGACY

Think about these questions for a few moments: What do I want my legacy to be? What do I want to leave behind that can live after me? According to Merriam-Webster, the word *legacy* means: a gift by will especially of money or other personal property; bequest. 'She left us a legacy of a million dollars.' Something transmitted by or received from an ancestor or predecessor or from the past. Other synonyms are: bequest, inheritance, heritage, endowment, settlement, or birthright.

Proverbs 13:22 says, *"A good man leaves an inheritance for his children's children."* If we go back now to the very first chapter of this book, did we all concur that God is the owner of everything? Well, if you agree with that while you are living, how about when you die, whose is it then? Should you

LEGACY! - PROVERBS 13:22
"A good man leaves an inheritance for his children's children."

possibly give some serious thought to how much of your estate holdings should or could go into something that could live on long after you die? Granted, one's legacy is much more than land, or dollars and cents. It is a life lived and invested in God's Kingdom, one's family, friends, and more.

However, there could be significant opportunity to also invest monetarily in some things that could give lasting influence for good for decades and even generations to come. So, what are you passionate about? Possibly missions work, Christian education, helping to fight poverty and feed the hungry, grandchildren's education,

> **"A GOOD MAN LEAVES AN INHERITANCE FOR HIS CHILDREN'S CHILDREN."**
> Proverbs 13:22

your church's vision and purpose? Martin Luther said, "I have held many things in my hands and I have lost them all. But whatever I have placed in God's hands, that I still possess." In other words, *'naked I came into this world, and naked I shall leave.'* **Job 1:21** We came in empty handed and we will leave just the same. Remember, even Rockefeller left it ALL behind.

Alfred Nobel dropped the newspaper and put his head in his hands. It was 1888. Nobel was a Swedish chemist who made his fortune inventing and producing dynamite. His brother, Ludvig, had died in France. But now, Alfred's grief was compounded by dismay. He had just read an obituary in a French newspaper – not his brother's obituary, but HIS! An editor had confused the brothers. The headline read, "The Merchant of Death is Dead". Alfred Nobel's obituary described a man who had become rich by helping people kill one another. Shaken by this appraisal of his life, Nobel resolved to use his wealth to change his legacy. When he died eight years later, he left more than $9 million to fund awards for people whose work benefited humanity. These awards became known as the Nobel Prizes. Alfred Nobel had a rare opportunity – to look at the assessment of his life at its end and still have the chance to change it. Before his life was over, Nobel made sure he invested his wealth in something of lasting value. He was able to change his legacy in this world.

If you are interested in leaving a financial legacy as well as your family and spiritual legacies, there are some pretty innovative ways to do it with or without a huge outlay. One of the ways I think you should look into is to leverage your investments utilizing life insurance. Many times, when people hear the word life insurance their reaction is: I don't want anybody "selling" me life insurance. I don't want it and I don't need it. For whatever reason, there seems to be some negative bias towards this product. Many people seem to think if they get life insurance, it's a bad omen they are going to die sooner because they admitted their mortality. Yes, it's true there are folks out there who just want to make a commission and 'sell' you insurance you don't want or need, but that doesn't mean that the product itself is always bad. It's not. There are some very good uses for insurance, if utilized to solve the right problems.

I love helping families solve problems and to provide solutions. That being the case, there are certainly times when properly utilized life insurance is a great solution. In fact, let me tell you about a couple I know, let's call them Jim and Jane. Jim and Jane are 66 years old, and have a very nice nest egg with investments worth $2 million. Everything is paid for and they have a comfortable income from a pension, and both Social Security checks. Their $2 million investments are providing an average return of approximately 6% annually, which is an additional $120,000 of interest/income. Most years they only use about $30,000 of that interest to live on or take a vacation. The rest of the money made yearly is just re-invested. Jim and Jane are involved in mission trips through their church and are very generous givers who dream of ways to leverage their God-given nest egg for His Kingdom. I was able to show them how they could take $30,000 per year (which represents 1.5% of their investment net-worth) and fund a Survivorship Universal Life (SUL) insurance policy. This could provide a legacy gift to the charity or mission of their choice of $2 million. In other words, they are able to take just a portion of their interest earned each year on their nest egg and, essentially, DOUBLE the size of their legacy gifts! WOW! They were overjoyed. What's great also is that this doesn't affect their lifestyle or retirement dreams in any way in the meantime. This couple spent weeks dreaming of all the ways this extra $2 million could enhance Kingdom work and things they are very passionate about. Finally, they decided they would leave $800,000 of that money to a Haiti missions project; $600,000 to the small Christian college that Jim had graduated from; and $600,000 to their local church; specifically to the future children's ministry. How cool is that? I think it's very cool! And guess what? This is something nearly every family could do in some capacity whether you have a smaller or larger nest-egg than Jim and Jane. What I would tell you is that this isn't the only way, but it's truly a very good way. It's one way that my wife,

Ginnie, and I have chosen to increase our legacy investments for Kingdom building in the future as well.

There are certainly other methods and aspects to building and leaving a lasting legacy. The question you need to ask yourself is: "What do I want my spiritual, family, financial, and intellectual legacy to be?" The truth is, each of us is building our legacy every day either intentionally or otherwise. As with all the components covered in this book, it's best to have a plan - a plan with a purpose.

IX. GET HELP AND ACCOUNTABILITY

The modern world of money management and investing is increasingly complex.   The investment and insurance options are virtually endless and they keep changing. We are now much more globally connected in our economy and stock market. Tax laws seem to grow in complexity every time congress meets, and changes in the economy can have significant impact on your financial goals.

As I sit here and write this section of the book, our country is in the middle of some significant proposed changes regarding the financial world and taxes. Let's say for our conversation that all the proposed changes go through; will those changes be permanent? They won't, will they? Eventually, a new administration will come in and make changes they feel are better than the current ones. How to

BE PREPARED! - PROVERBS 20:18
Solomon says: "Make plans by seeking advice; if you wage war, obtain guidance."

navigate the current economy, tax laws, and changing investment options will continue to be a moving target for investors and families.

KEY AREAS THAT IMPACT YOUR LIFETIME FINANCIAL
FREEDOM AND SECURITY INCLUDE:

- Retirement Planning
- Estate Planning
- Budgeting
- Investment Choices
- Risk Management
- Tax Planning

We strongly recommend that you don't try to do this on your own. Solomon says in **Proverbs 20:18**, *"Make plans by seeking advice; if you wage war, obtain guidance."* If you needed surgery, you wouldn't mail order a scalpel and attempt to do your own life-saving surgery. That would be foolish. What you do is start looking for the best surgeon money can buy, and put your life in their hands.

> **"MAKE PLANS BY SEEKING ADVICE; IF YOU WAGE WAR, OBTAIN GUIDANCE."**
> Proverbs 20:18

When undertaking any endeavor, whether business, personal, or financial, deciding who you will partner with is crucial to the success of the venture. Choosing the right financial advisor can make the difference between having a happy, confident, worry-free retirement, and one fraught with concern. Just as finding the right match in most any undertaking is important to its success, the firm you select to assist you with your financial future needs to be a good match. The people you work with must have your interest at heart and share your values. The decision, of course, is a personal one, but there are several criteria that it would be prudent to consider in making it. Here are a few:

1. ARE THEY INDEPENDENT?

What you don't want to do, in most cases, is select a financial advisor who is an employee of a large "brokerage" firm. Whose interests do you think that individual will be representing – yours or the employer? Virtually anyone can hang a sign advertising himself or herself as a financial advisor. They may be able to offer a few solutions to your financial problems, but at the end of the trail, the solutions will usually result in you buying products that the company is selling. The managers tell their "advisors" what funds to recommend to clients, not because these funds are necessarily what you need to have to reach your investment goals, but because selling them benefits the brokerage house. The advisor's job is not necessarily to enhance your financial situation, but to increase the value of the company's stock shares and enhance the pocketbooks of shareholders. There is nothing illegal about this. Like any other enterprise in America, they are in business to make a profit. If you choose a Wall Street brokerage firm as your advisor, you are unlikely to find individuals who will educate and inform you, and then allow you to make independent choices. An independent advisor's one single obligation is to you and you only.

2. Are You Dealing with a Fiduciary?

Now, there's a word you don't use very often in everyday conversation. What does it mean? The word "fiduciary" comes from the Latin word, "fiduciarius", meaning, "to hold in trust". The word connotes *a legal or ethical relationship of trust between two or more parties.* The root word of "fiduciary" is the Latin "fides," which means true. Cousin words that share the same root are "confidential," "fidelity" and "bona fide", all of which have to do with faithfulness and trust.

In the financial world, a fiduciary has pledged to work for the interests of his or her client, and swears to put that client's interests ahead of his or her own. The advice fiduciaries give must always be client-driven as opposed to profit-driven. The best type of fiduciary is a Registered Investment Advisory Firm (RIA). This simply means that financial professionals within this firm have made an official pledge, at the risk of losing their license and their livelihood, to place their client's interests ahead of their own, without exception. Registered Investment Advisory firms are audited regularly by state and/or federal government securities regulators to ensure that this is happening.

3. DO THEY UNDERSTAND YOU?

Have you ever noticed that when you visit the doctor's office for your annual physical exam, the nurse hands you a clipboard with several forms to fill out? It may irritate you to have to fill them out again when you gave the same information last year, but the forms are necessary. Your health situation may have changed in the last 12 months. The doctor will ask you several questions during the face-to-face portion of the exam, too. Why? Because a good physician will want to know everything about you, physically, before they treat you. A competent doctor would never prescribe medication for you without first having a complete understanding of your physical condition, and knowing any other medication you are taking. A competent financial advisor will be one who takes the time to thoroughly understand your financial situation. He or she will spend time listening to you in order to ascertain not only what your financial goals are, but why. A competent financial advisor will formulate a plan to execute your wishes. You want to work with a financial advisor who has no product to push and no other agenda to follow except yours.

4. Do They Think Like You?

By this we don't mean that they must agree with you on personal issues or share your taste in music and entertainment. Of course not! But when it comes to your money it is crucial that they share your values. If you are nearing, or in retirement, your resources are precious to you because of what they represent: independence and quality of life. If you are not willing to treat those assets as if they were fodder for the gambling casinos in Las Vegas, then neither should they. And yet we have heard horror stories where that appears to have been the case – advisors who are insensitive to the age of their clients and where they are along the financial timeline. If you are like most folks in the red zone of retirement, you have a path in mind. You need advisors who will accompany you and help you over the obstacles in that path – not ones who will attempt to lead you to a different path just because it is one more familiar to them. Let us give you an example:

In our RIA firm, our goal is to preserve wealth and putting assets to work in such a way that your income is supplemented without depleting your principle, where possible. When potential clients come to our office for a consultation, the first thing we do is chat. We want to know what is on their mind. What are their notions about money and finances? We want to be able to match our thinking with theirs so we can work together. But if we can't, there is no need to proceed. We part as friends, but we are not a match for everyone and we do not try to be.

Sometimes we find it useful to ask potential clients to pretend that all their money was cash and stacked up in their living room. Sounds crazy, but it helps put things in perspective. Here's all this money; what should you do with it? You can't just leave it there. If you invest it, what should be the primary attribute of this investment? What do you want the money to do for you and your family? If you are near or at retirement age your priorities might be in this order:

- Safety
- Growth/Income
- Fees
- Tax efficiencies
- Liquidity

For those in this phase of life, it's not how much money you make, but how much of it you keep that counts, in most cases. What benefit is there in growing your wealth, only to let it slip away?

However, for most investors who are 20-50 years old their priorities could look like this:

- High risk growth
- Low fees
- Tax efficiencies
- Liquidity
- Safety

5. HOW ARE THEY COMPENSATED?

In your search for the right advisor be sure to find out how the advisor candidate is paid. If you are paying them, then they work for you. If a brokerage house, or some other major firm, is paying them, they don't work for you. It's as simple as that; they work for someone else. Don't be embarrassed to ask, "How are you compensated?" That is not a personal question; it is a business question. It is appropriate fact-finding. You are not asking that to be nosy or to find out the advisor's yearly salary or net worth. You want to know if there are possible conflicts of interest or hidden fees and charges. Knowing how your advisor is compensated may help you understand and evaluate how objective he or she will be in any recommendations you receive. True professionals will not mind this dialogue between client and advisor at all.

6. HOW WILL THEY WORK WITH YOU?

There should be a high level of communication between you and your financial advisor. Do not hesitate to ask what the firm's policy is on periodic reviews of your portfolio. Also, ask who will be handling your account? Will it be farmed out to a third-party firm or given to a rookie associate to manage? Or, will the advisor candidate you are interviewing be the one who personally handles the account. If other team members will be involved in managing your account, wouldn't it be a good idea to meet and get to know them?

When you dial the office phone number will a human answer the phone during business hours, or will you have to listen to a series of impersonal prompts that ask you to enter information repeatedly, only to then be connected to someone's voice mail? We know many of you are computer literate and up to date on modern technology. But you may get frustrated when you have to press one for English or two for Spanish and then digitally enter your date of birth, pin number, account number and zip code, only to have to listen to another menu of choices. When it comes to your money, you need to have personal contact.

7. HOW MUCH EXPERIENCE DO THEY HAVE?

If you are like most people, you don't relish the idea of being a guinea pig. Don't hesitate to ask how long your advisor candidate has been counseling clients. Ask about their experience. How did their clients fare in the last market crash? How successful has your advisor candidate been at providing solutions that ensure guaranteed income for his or her clients in retirement? Ask what services the firm offers. Are they able to offer a well-rounded approach, or is their focus so narrow that they only know one path? Abraham Maslow said, "If the only tool you have is a hammer, you tend to see every problem as a nail." Are they holistic in their approach to financial planning?

Holistic medical treatment involves treating the "whole" person. Likewise, holistic financial planning refutes the one-size-fits-all approach. It is comprehensive planning that looks beyond rate of return and addresses the end goals of the client. Some call it "life planning" with an emphasis on the financial. More and more people want to make sure that their money will do what they want it to do. Holistic planning involves every aspect of your financial life. It is based on the idea that your money should have a purpose. Otherwise, it is merely numbers on paper.

Some people come into the offices of Beacon Capital Management and know exactly what they want to do with their wealth. With those clients, we become facilitators. We help them execute their plan. Other folks don't really know what they want. With them, our work is that of educators. We help them visualize the future and translate the possible application of their resources to their individual personal circumstances. If it sounds corny to talk in terms of people's deepest needs, goals, desires and dreams, we don't apologize. As "touchy-feely" as that sounds, when it's your life, it takes on a different feel altogether.

Holistic planning takes a multi-disciplinary approach to financial planning and involves developing a team of professionals who can deliver investment, retirement, and estate planning estate. All advisor teams should include a financial planner, a CPA, and an Estate Planning Attorney. Key players, in addition to those, could include a Business Attorney, Certified Valuation Analyst (CVA), Investment Broker, Insurance Agent, Business Broker, etc. However, coordinating such a team can be daunting and intimidating for the client, so the Holistic Planner acts as the liaison between the client and the advisor team.

What other services do they offer? Service is important in financial planning. How often will they meet with you to discuss your progress? The financial landscape is constantly changing. Your needs and your thinking may change, too. You need to meet with your advisory firm at least once a year, maybe more often than that, to keep pace with these changes.

Lastly, do you like this person? What is your gut telling you about this person? Don't ignore this. Your instinct is mostly right in measuring trust. Feelings, after all, are facts. Do you feel that you can trust this individual to be an advocate for you in this important area of life?

8. RETAIL VERSUS INSTITUTIONAL INVESTING

As everyone knows, it's better for the old wallet if you can get it wholesale. When it comes to investing, large corporations and institutions are at an advantage when it comes to pricing and selection. There is no reason why smaller investors cannot enjoy that same advantage. It all depends on the financial advisor you choose.

There is a tremendous advantage when ordinary folks have the services of institutional-level advisors and consultants. These professionals can often help investors to bypass the additional costs of the retail brokerage market. Institutional account holders generally trade directly without the extra costs associated with retail distribution and marketing. Call it cutting out the middle man if you wish, and, in the bargain, getting someone who will tell you the truth, the whole truth, and nothing but the truth about your financial affairs. Individual investors who receive institutional-level advice, benefit from having professional managers and financial planners focusing on their overall allocation and the active movement of capital to attractive areas from unattractive ones. It's the difference between active management and the staid "buy-and-hold" philosophy of investing that is no longer an effective way to navigate the risks presented by today's geographically diverse, fast-paced financial markets. This is especially true for retirees. Of all investor classes, these folks are making critical allocation decisions with the portion of their portfolios they place in the stock market. They deserve full-time, institutional-level professionals working on their behalf and to be directly accountable when making the really important investment allocation decisions.

IT'S WORTH THE EFFORT

Selecting the right advisor will require some work on your part, but it's worth it when you consider just how critical your decisions about money are when you are preparing for retirement. Getting it right is the difference between losing sleep and having peace of mind. Selecting the right guide for this part of your financial journey can mean being able to enjoy your golden years instead of worrying about them. Let's face it – retirement is unfamiliar territory. There is the possibility for great adventure but also potential danger if you fail to prepare properly. To make sure you take the right steps, you want a guide who knows the landscape and can get you through it safely with enough money for the rest of your life.

In addition to getting help and accountability by selecting the right coach or advisor, you also should diligently look for an accountability partner to

YOU SHOULD DILIGENTLY LOOK FOR AN ACCOUNTABILITY PARTNER TO ENCOURAGE YOU AND TO MOTIVATE YOU TO SET AND ACCOMPLISH YOUR FINANCIAL GOALS.

encourage you and to motivate you to set and accomplish your financial goals. I suggest meeting with this person specifically about this either bi-weekly or at least monthly. This step will be critical to your financial success!

X.   EXCEL AT GIVING

People, by nature, love to give! Seriously, let's think about

Christmas Eve. You have children or grandchildren and, (especially when they were young) how excited were you to GIVE them special gifts they had asked for? Not only are kids anxious for Christmas morning, oftentimes the parents are even more impatient and eager. Let's face it, giving is fun and it's addicting, and there is a feeling it gives you that is difficult to measure or express. Which Oprah or Ellen shows get the highest ratings? You guessed it, the ones when they give away cars to all the audience members. A few months later you can look and see how many views those shows received on You-tube.   It

GIVING! - 1 CORINTHIANS 9:7
"Each man should give what he has decided in his heart to give, not reluctantly or under compulsion, for God loves a cheerful giver."

can be in the millions. The Bible calls us to be givers. **2 Corinthians 8:7**– *"See that you also <u>excel</u> in the grace of giving…"* **Proverbs 3:9** – *"Honor the Lord with your wealth, with the first fruits of all your crops; then your barns will be filled to overflowing and your vats will brim over with new wine."* **Luke 6:38** – *<u>Give</u> and it will be given to you. A good measure, pressed down, shaken together and running over will be poured into your lap."* **1 Timothy 6:18-19** – *"Be rich in good deeds, and <u>generous</u> and willing to share…. you will lay up treasure for yourself as a firm foundation for the coming age."* **1 Corinthians 9:7**, *"Each man should give what he has decided in his heart to give, not reluctantly or under compulsion, for God loves a <u>cheerful giver</u>."*

God owns everything and doesn't need us to give to Him but He asks us to give and allows us the joy of giving. It's such a blessing and honor to give to God and His work. Pete Wilson, former Pastor of Cross Point church in Nashville TN, once stated in a sermon, "Make money a tool for good, not a drug for yourself." Jesus made these comments: *"If you're honest in small things, you'll be honest in big things; If you're a crook in small things,*

> ## "YOU MAKE A LIVING BY WHAT YOU GET - YOU MAKE A LIFE BY WHAT YOU GIVE!"
> Winston Churchill

you'll be a crook in big things. If you're not honest in small jobs, who will put you in charge of the store? No worker can serve two bosses: He'll either hate the first and love the second or adore the first and despise the second. You can't serve both God and the Bank." **Luke 16:10-13 MSG** Give money away! It is truly one of life's greatest pleasures. Give to others. Winston Churchill penned these words, "You make a living by what you get – you make a life by what you give!"

Also, giving has nothing to do with how much money you make or have. In the late 1990s, Americans were 400% richer, after taxes and inflation, than in the Great Depression, yet giving ranged from 1.9% to 2.6%. In 1933, the depth of the Great Depression, giving was 3.2%! Tithing is a Biblical principle. **Malachi 3:8-10**, *"Will a man rob God? Yet you rob me. But you ask, 'how do we rob you?' In tithes and offerings. You are under a curse – the whole nation of you – because you are robbing me. Bring the whole tithe into the storehouse, that there may be food in my house. 'Test me in this', says the Lord Almighty, and see if I will not throw open the floodgates of heaven and pour out so much blessing that you will not have room enough for it."* Now there are some who believe that as long as we give our 10% tithe, then we have license to do whatever we want as Christians with the other 90%. Bill Hybels says, "The tithe is a wonderful goal, but a terrible place to stop!"[18] I believe that the Bible teaches very clearly that 100% of all that we make, all that we have, all that we will get in the future is God's. We will be held accountable one day not just for the 10% but for 100% of all our income and possessions. When asked whether a Christian should tithe off of the gross or on the net, one man said, "Well, it depends, do you want to be "grossly" blessed by God or "netly" blessed by God?"

FIVE CATEGORIES OF GIVING:

1. **Random Tipper**- This is the person in life who feels a very mild tug to give to things occasionally, so he pacifies that feeling by giving a few dollars every now and then, mostly just so he can convince himself that he gives.

2. **Regular Contributor**- This person is compelled to give to charities, causes, and their church quite regularly. There is no set amount, and sometimes it's not much, but they are a regular giver to needs that grip them.

3. **Resolute Tither**- This person takes the verses in the Bible on tithing very, very seriously. They give a 10th of their income religiously. They would never think of missing out and if not at church on a particular Sunday, they always make it up. To them this is one of God's commands and expectations and they can be counted on to give their tithe each and every week.

4. **Radical Giver**- Now this person takes this giving experience to a whole new level. This person feels the need and pull to give beyond what is seen as the tithe (10%). They give over and above that continually: to missions, to local charities, to people and causes they see around them and around the world, and look for opportunities to give way over and above what is normal.

5. **Ridiculously Generous**- This person is highly extreme in their giving. They would be viewed as 'over the top' in their life of generosity, even to the point of taking it to ridiculous levels. At this level, we are talking about people who would sacrifice greatly to give excessive amounts of money. This person may even give 50%, 60%, 70%, or even a higher

amount of their income to charities, churches, people, and causes on a very regular basis. It has become a lifestyle. Instead of lavish living, it's all about lavish giving!

Here's a question to consider: Which of those five categories would you put God into? Is God a random tipper? Is he a regular contributor? Or is God ridiculously generous? I believe He is the latter. **John 3:16**, *"For God so loved the world, He GAVE his one and only Son (Jesus)...."* He gave us His very own son, to die for our sins so that we could live in heaven one day with Him. I'd certainly say that God is <u>ridiculously generous.</u>   So, when are we most like Jesus? We are most like Jesus when we take what the world worships (money) and we generously sow it into His Kingdom and Kingdom work. **Proverbs 22:9** – *"A generous man will himself be blessed, for he shares his food with the poor."* **2 Corinthians 9:6 & 7** - *"Remember this: Whoever sows sparingly will also reap sparingly, and whoever sows generously, will also reap generously."*   You see, the world is focused on radical <u>consumption</u>, and God calls His followers to radical contribution. What again is the antidote to our culture's love for money and things? It is contentment and giving money away. Generosity isn't an event or a simple act of giving. Generosity is a lifestyle that changes hearts and minds as it blesses everyone involved. I have learned over

> **GENEROSITY IS A LIFESTYLE THAT CHANGES HEARTS AND MINDS AS IT BLESSES EVERYONE INVOLVED.**

the years that giving is the most fun you can have with money. And I have to say, I am hooked. And oh, by the way, generosity shouldn't be a pressure, but instead it should be a privilege!!! Don't give out of coercion, give from a heart of love. The tithe belongs to God. It's not ours to do as we wish. It's His money. He just asks us to give it back to Him, to see if we will be obedient. **Matthew 6: 19-21**, *"Do not store up for yourselves treasures on earth, where moth and rust destroy, and where thieves break in and steal. But store for yourselves treasures in heaven, where moth and rust do not destroy, and where thieves do not break in and steal. For where your treasure is, there your heart will be also."* Randy Alcorn gives what I believe to be the best analogy of **Matthew 6:19-21** when he states, "Imagine you are alive at the end of the Civil War. You're living in the South, but you are a Northerner. You plan to move home as soon as the war is over. While in the South you've accumulated lots of Confederate currency. Now, suppose you know for a fact that the North is going to win the war and the end is imminent. What will you do with your Confederate money? If you're smart, there's only one answer. You should immediately cash in your Confederate currency for U.S. currency – the only money that will have value once the war is over. Keep only enough Confederate currency to meet your short-term needs. As a Christian, you have inside knowledge of an eventual worldwide upheaval caused by Christ's return. This is the ultimate insider trading tip – earth's currency will become worthless when Christ returns – or when you die, whichever comes first (either event could happen at any time)." Alcorn goes on to state what he calls the Treasure Principle, "You can't take it with you, but you can send it on ahead."[19]

One of the heroes of the Christian faith is a missionary by the name of Jim Elliot. Elliot was one of the missionaries killed in 1956 by Auca Indians. In his biography, "Shadow of the Almighty", Jim says, "He is no fool who gives what he cannot keep, to gain that which he cannot lose."[20] Be prepared and surprised by God's unexpected methods of blessing and the size of that blessings. Don't limit God. He has ways and means to bless you financially that you could have never imagined.   God is calling us to a life of generosity: generous with our time, our talents, and our treasures. He calls us:

A. when we have little…. even when we are poor. **2 Corinthians 8:2-4** *"…. for in a severe test of affliction, their abundance of joy and their extreme poverty have overflowed in a wealth of generosity on their part. For they gave according to their means, as I can testify, and beyond their means, of their own accord, begging earnestly for the favor of taking part in the relief of the saints…."* Wow, can you hear this? Even when they were dirt poor and in severe financial hardship, they were begging for a chance to participate in giving to the cause of Christ! Amazing.

B. when we have much…. when we are rich. **1 Timothy 6:17-19**, *"Command those who are rich in this present world not to be arrogant nor to put their hope in wealth, which is so uncertain, but to put their hope in God, who richly provides us with everything for our enjoyment. Command them to do good, to be rich in good deeds, and to be generous and willing to share. In this way, they will lay up treasure for themselves as a firm foundation for the coming age, so that they may take hold of the life that is truly life."*

XI. TOP THREE TAKEAWAYS

1. YOU HAVE NO CHOICE BUT TO LEARN ABOUT MONEY

Having money in life to support you and your family is not optional. This is not one of those things you can just decide yay or nay about. Money is essential for all families to pay the bills and take care of them. Eating broccoli is a choice. Liking football is a choice (well, maybe not here in the South). Personal hygiene is not a choice! Having money to pay bills is not a choice. Therefore, learning about it is also not a choice. You will either learn the wrong ways to handle money, either accidently or on purpose, or you will learn the right ways to handle money. Why not learn the right ways? It really is quite simple; it's just not easy. Hopefully this book can continue to be a source of information and inspiration as you continue on your journey with finances.

2. TREAT YOUR FAMILY FINANCES LIKE A BUSINESS

Running your financial household is very similar to running a business. What if a business didn't have a business plan, didn't ever have board meetings or other planning meetings, and what if they never kept track of income and expenses? How successful would it be? Likely your answer, like mine, would be the same: not very! There's a strong chance that business would fail.

If your family household income is $25,000 per year and you live for 60 years as an adult (age 20 to age 80), then you have been entrusted with $1.5 million during your lifetime. If your family income averages $50,000 then it's $3 million; if $100K then it's $6 million. If a company's budget is $1 million, $3 million, or even $6 million, don't you agree they should have monthly or quarterly business meetings, and shouldn't they have a budget, with detailed tracking? Well, guess what, that's your situation. Why not plan on having an annual family business meeting in early January where you talk about the past year with its financial successes and failures? In the meeting, you should lay out in writing this new year's short-term, mid-term, and long-term financial goals. Along with that, look at your income and expenses and make necessary adjustments. Also as a family, divide up the various financial duties for the year. Be sure to set a date and time for each family meeting for the year, and put it on the calendar. At a minimum, these need to be held monthly.

3. BE DIFFERENT/ABNORMAL

It is a fact that many individuals and families do not follow the principles of this book. In fact, the vast majority do not. Also, most families are struggling financially. They do not have a plan; they do not have a budget; they do not track expenses; they do not live within or below their means; do not have proper amounts of insurance; have not been investing enough for their future retirement; and unfortunately they can't be nearly as generous as they would like as a result of this. If this is normal, I, for one, want to be abnormal. How about you? Someone once said, "watch the habits of broke people and do the opposite." Dave Ramsey has coined the phrase, "normal is broke."[21] Don't float downstream with most of the fish, turn around and swim upstream. Be different! Be abnormal. Most of the habits we have picked up about money, are bad habits. Dare to be different. Adopt new habits and new methods in your finances. These new habits will pay HUGE dividends.

In closing, our prayer for this book is that you will get to experience what it is like to go from financial failure to financial fitness!

NOTES

[1]"Jim Rohn Quotes." Quotes.net. STANDS4 LLC, 2017. Web. 4 Sep. 2017. <http://www.quotes.net/quote/17017>.

[2]Zig Ziglar Quotes. (n.d.). BrainyQuote.com. https://www.brainyquote.com/quotes/quotes/z/zigziglar173503.html

[3]Jim Rohn Quotes. (n.d.). BrainyQuote.com https://www.brainyquote.com/quotes/quotes/j/jimrohn393427.html

[4]Mark Twain Quotes. (n.d.). BrainyQuote.com. https://www.brainyquote.com/quotes/quotes/m/marktwain118964.html

[5]Alice's Adventure in Wonderland, Macmillian, November 26, 1865

[6]Yogi Berra Quotes. (n.d.). BrainyQuote.com. Retrieved September 4, 2017, from BrainyQuote.com Web site: https://www.brainyquote.com/quotes/quotes/y/yogiberra391900.html

[7]Tyranny of the Urgent by Charles Hummel. Copyright 1967 by InterVarsity Christian Fellowship of the USA. InterVarsity Press, P.O. Box 1400, Downers Grove, IL 60515.

[8]Sermon 50 "The Use of Money" in The Works of the Reverend John Wesley, A.M. (1840) edited by John Emory, Vol. I, p. 446

[9]Jim Rohn Quotes. (n.d.). BrainyQuote.com. https://www.brainyquote.com/quotes/quotes/j/jimrohn132691.html

[10]Hill, Napoleon (1953). Think and Grow Rich. Cleveland, Ohio: The Ralston Publishing Co.

[11]Saint Augustine Quotes. (n.d.). BrainyQuote.com https://www.brainyquote.com/quotes/quotes/s/saintaugus165165.html

[12]John Maxwell shared this thought while at the Stewardship Challenge conference in Baltimore, MD on November 9th.

[13]http://lhim.org/blog/2012/10/02/tim-keller-identifying-idols/

[14]The Wealthy Barber: The Common Sense Guide to Successful Financial Planning. Toronto: Stoddart. 1989. ISBN 0-7737-5318-4.

[15]http://www.quotesonfinance.com/quote/79/Albert-Einstein-Compound-interest

[16]The Compound Effect (pg.10,11), Published by Vanguard Press, 387 Park Avenue South, 12th floor, New York, NY10016

[17]Making the Most of Your Money Now: Simon & Schuster | 1264 pages | ISBN 9780743269964 | December 2009

[18]https://www.egsnetwork.com/pages/stewardship.php?p=6

[19]The Treasure Principle, Trust Media Oto (2005) English ISBN-10: 1415820155

ISBN-13: 978-1415820155

[19]In The Shadow of the Almighty, published by Harper and Row in 1958.

[21]Twitter: April 29, 2014 @DaveRamsey

ABOUT THE AUTHORS

C. PETE BENSON

Pete grew up on Grand Manan Island, New Brunswick, Canada, an island of quaint fishing villages about as far removed from the hubbub of urban life as you can get.

Pete's father was a lobster fisherman and his grandfather owned a herring processing plant where Pete worked growing up.

Pete learned early on that the life of a fisherman was not for him. On his first serious outing with his father he discovered he was chronically prone to seasickness.

Pete is the founder and co-owner of Beacon Capital Management with his business partner, Jon Maxson. Together they have built a very successful, and comprehensive Wealth Management firm that is well-recognized in the Middle Tennessee area and beyond. Their TV show called "Beacon Retirement Strategies" is shown weekly on the local Nashville NBC and CBS channels and also their one hour weekly radio show by the same name airs on 99.7 Supertalk in Nashville and around middle TN. Additionally, Pete has been a featured guest on Fox Business, CNBC the Closing Bell, CNBC Asia, and in Yahoo Finance, Minyanville, Reuter's and more. Pete has authored three other books and is a frequent guest speaker at financial conferences to other Advisors, at District and Denominational events, Camp meetings, Christian colleges, and churches across the U.S. and Canada.

Pete is literally married to the "girl next door," Ginnie, who was his high school sweetheart. They grew up seven houses apart. Ginnie's and Pete's parents were friends, and the two families attended the same small church in the same small village. They have been married 41 years and are parents to three children, Ginger, Amanda, and Dan (co-author of this book), and have seven grandchildren. Pete and Ginnie are dual citizens of the United States and Canada. They raised their family in Canada for the early years and then moved South in 1989. Pete and Ginnie live in Franklin, Tennessee, a rapidly growing suburb of Nashville.

Daniel P. J. Benson

Dan's heart for others was obvious from a very young age. He has always had a special way with people of all ages and his genuine care and concern are always evident in how he communicates to people.

Dan is a born leader in life and in the many sports teams he has been part of.

After graduating high school in the year 2000, Dan attended Southern Wesleyan University where he was the captain of the men's soccer team. It was here that Dan developed his passion for helping people and families with their finances.

In the summer of 2002, Dan participated in an internship at Beacon Capital Management where he spent the summer learning about the business from his father, Pete. When the internship was over and he headed back to university, he knew that his career would bring him back to Beacon.

Dan now serves as the Executive Vice President at Beacon Capital Management as well as being a leading Financial Advisor at the firm where he helps families find financial freedom and gain confidence in their retirement plan. He listens to their needs and then builds custom financial plans to meet their goals and objectives.

Dan is a dedicated husband to his wife Mandy and a father of three children, Kayleigh, Connor and Imogen, his pride and joy. He is passionate about his faith and his responsibility to use the platform and gifts God has given him to enhance the lives of others.

The time Dan has spent in the financial industry, his education and most importantly his upbringing by two Godly role models, serves as the foundation of his passion to help others.

48440012R00074

Made in the USA
Columbia, SC
12 January 2019